HOPE for the FUTURE

Inspiring Women's Stories Showing the Way

Dr AMANDA NICKSON

First published by Ultimate World Publishing 2024
Copyright © 2024 Amanda Nickson

ISBN

Paperback: 978-1-923255-11-1
Ebook: 978-1-923255-12-8

Amanda Nickson has asserted her rights under the Copyright, Designs and Patents Act 1988 to be identified as the author of this work. The information in this book is based on the author's experiences and opinions. The publisher specifically disclaims responsibility for any adverse consequences which may result from use of the information contained herein. Permission to use information has been sought by the author. Any breaches will be rectified in further editions of the book.

All rights reserved. No part of this publication may be reproduced, stored in or introduced into a retrieval system, or transmitted in any form, or by any means (electronic, mechanical, photocopying, recording or otherwise) without the prior written permission of the author. Any person who does any unauthorised act in relation to this publication may be liable to criminal prosecution and civil claims for damages. Enquiries should be made through the publisher.

Cover design: Ultimate World Publishing
Layout and typesetting: Ultimate World Publishing
Editor: Alex Floyd-Douglass
Cover Photo: Amanda Nickson, Sunrise, Central Australia

Ultimate World Publishing
Diamond Creek,
Victoria Australia 3089
www.writeabook.com.au

Testimonials

"Not only is Amanda qualified to speak into the area of overcoming and having hope for the future, but she exemplifies a life where this is her default position. She radiates joy regardless of the circumstances and it's evident that there is a depth of not only knowledge but vast experience that enables her to speak to others and encourage them on their journey."

Jo Geerling, Senior Pastor, iSee Church

"I am very honoured to introduce Amanda as a genuine and true friend, a fellow traveller, living an abundant life of genuine faith in a big God. Despite experiencing seasons in her life of pain and suffering, moments of despair and discouragements, Amanda's personal testimony of learning to overcome against all odds, is a remarkable testament of faith and hope for the future in a big and loving God."

Emeritus. Rev. Emmanuel Fave (M.A. in Th/Min)
Pastor, Teacher, Church Leader and
Missionary at-Large

"When I became a Christian, I said that I had invited Jesus into my life, my story. However, the reality was that becoming a Christian was the moment I realised that I am part of God's amazing story that begins in a garden (Genesis 1) and ends in a city (Revelation 21–22), and which is all about Jesus and his kingdom. The Bible is full of stories: of complicated people depending on a God who steadfastly loves them. Jesus told stories: stories that made people laugh, get upset, be full of wonder, or simply be stunned at his wisdom. Stories are how we learn, they are the foundation of our relationships, and they inspire us. Amanda Nickson has gathered some incredible stories together. I challenge you to try and stop reading this book. They are stories of joy, heartbreak, hope and deep understanding. Stories shape us, and these stories will help you become more like Jesus."

Kara Martin, Mentor, Speaker,
Adjunct Professor and Author of Workship

"Having had the privilege of reading Amanda's earlier books, I was inspired by her character and prose. I can attest to the fact that this book is profound, inspiring and impactful. Through heartfelt narratives, Amanda beautifully captures the resilience, courage and triumphs of women from diverse backgrounds. Each story serves as a beacon of hope and empowerment, inspiring readers to embrace their own journeys with newfound strength and determination. Amanda's passion for uplifting women shines through every page, making this a book a must-read for anyone seeking inspiration and motivation."

Kelly Markey, Bestselling and Award-Winning Author,
Ambassador of Hope, Publisher

"When I think of Dr. Amanda Nickson, I am reminded of sunshine. But this is not ordinary sunshine, it is that sunshine that breaks through a cloudy and rainy day, to turn the sky into the most beautiful blue. It's a blue that not only beautifies the skies, but a blue that gives hope to all those who look up to catch a glimpse of its loveliness. I have known Amanda for almost 20 years now. Over the years, I have had the opportunity of understanding that life hasn't been always easy for her. Against all odds, she has continued to surely and steadily defeat her mountains, one of which is her well-deserved PhD degree which she completed eight years ago. Amanda is a true picture of hope, and a gift to all those who may have given up on their dreams, a gift that is living proof, that all things are possible."

**Pastor Ulemu Nyasulu,
Streams International Church**

Disclaimer

Some of the following stories in this book raise serious issues that happen in life. For anyone who has experienced trauma and can be triggered reading about childhood abuse, domestic and family violence, suicide, severe injuries, medical conditions, disabilities, death and loss, the introduction gives a brief overview of the types of issues covered in each chapter.

This disclaimer serves as a trigger warning. It is not the author's intention to cause any harm or distress by the stories in this book – quite the opposite. The author believes these stories will show women courageously moving forward to live in victory over differing circumstances and provide hope in the challenges life can throw us.

The author has made every effort to ensure that the information in this book was correct at the time of publication. However, the author and publisher accept no liability for any loss, damage or disruption incurred by the reader or any other person arising from any action taken or not taken based on the content of this book.

Dedication

To all the brave women over time who have defied the odds, moved forward and hoped and believed for a better future.

To all the women, who in the future, will take steps of faith with hope and expectation.

To my mother, Olive Middleton Wright, a courageous and inspiring woman who always had hope for a better future.

And to all the women who have inspired me.

Thank you.

Contents

Testimonials	iii
Disclaimer	vii
Dedication	ix
Introduction	1
Chapter 1: **Samantha Leonoski:** How Does Hope Bring Transformation?	5
Chapter 2 : **Karene Gravener:** He Will Make a Way Where There is No Way	21
Chapter 3: **Julie Mengel:** How Does Hope Bring Dreams and Possibilities to Life?	35
Chapter 4: **Sharon Henderson:** How Does Relying on God Bring Hope?	45
Chapter 5: **Ruth:** How Hope has Given Me a Future	57
Chapter 6: **Dr Rhonda Emonson:** How Does Hope Overcome Obstacles?	67
Chapter 7: **Dr Amanda Nickson:** How to Have Eternal Hope and Overcome the Impossible	75
Chapter 8: **Uma Rani Turimella:** How to Move from Despair to Hope	85

Chapter 9: **Jill Sutcliffe Everett:**
How We Can Have Hope Because God Has a Plan — 103

Chapter 10: **Jenni Sedon:**
How to Move From Hopelessness to Hope For the Future — 117

Chapter 11: **Soleil Nyirabyiza:**
How to Be Confident For the Future — 125

Chapter 12: **Ann-Marie McCann:**
How Hope Can Bring Provision — 135

Afterward — 147

Additional Information and Resources — 151

Discussion Questions For a Book Club or Discussion Group — 153

Biographies — 157

About the Author — 163

Other Books by the Author — 165

Acknowledgements — 167

Speaker Bio — 169

Offers — 171

Introduction

I have lived in Townsville in North Queensland for over 30 years. A while back, I was reflecting on the number of truly inspiring women I have met in Townsville; some in my local church, some in other churches and some as colleagues through my previous workplace. I was astounded and inspired by the resilience and tenacity of woman to keep going and to hold on to hope for a better future, even in overwhelming circumstances.

I decided I would approach these women and see if they would be prepared to share some of their life story to bring hope and inspiration to other people – perhaps struggling with their own challenges. I suggested I could interview them, transcribe their words and craft them into their chapter. A couple of the women opted to write their own stories without the interview process. Most have been interviewed and a version of their stories now makes up the chapters in this book in their own words.

We all need inspiration that hope is possible and that we can achieve amazing things – despite the challenges that can happen to us.

I want to sincerely thank the women who have been open about their life experiences and how hope has been part of their journey and for their bravery in sharing their personal challenges with readers. Their stories of how hope has evolved are found in each chapter, outlined here. Thank you:

- Samantha Leonoski, for your courage and determination overcoming childhood abuse, foster care and health challenges and thriving in life.
- Karene Gravener, for sharing your journey with Cerebral Palsy and being an advocate for others with disabilities.
- Julie Mengel, for your determination to never give up on your dreams as a single parent for many years, overcoming a difficult childhood and battling health issues.
- Sharon Henderson, for pressing into God after domestic violence, raising seven children as a single mother and caring for a child with multiple disabilities.
- Ruth*, for shifting from being a victim of childhood abuse to being an overcomer full of faith and peace with children with rare medical conditions.
- Rhonda Emonson, for moving forward with unexpected and life altering injuries to completing studies and now being able to share part of her story to encourage others.
- Amanda Nickson, for sharing your journey with dyslexia, anxiety and depression and a belief that you can do all things through Christ who strengthens you.
- Uma Rani Turimella, who has endured devastating grief during the COVID-19 pandemic, and yet has found that the joy of the Lord is her strength.
- Jill Sutcliffe Everett, who as a single female has boldly travelled to Iran and Turkey where God called her to missions, and has found her own path, defying some expectations.

---

* Ruth is a pseudonym chosen by one of the women in this book who wished to keep her identity private.

Introduction

- Jenni Seden, who has known the hopelessness of a loved one's suicide and has found comfort in a God who treasures her every tear.
- Soleil Nyirabyiza, who has known the isolation of moving to a new country as a refugee, struggled with cultural differences, trying to fit in and has found her confidence and identity in a renewed relationship with God.
- Ann-Marie McCann, who has learned to trust God for provision in tough circumstances and is eager to see what God has for her to do on her next assignment.

At the end of each woman's chapter, I have added a couple of questions to consider, which I trust will help make connections between the chapter, yourself and your situation.

Two verses continue to resonate with me on the topic of hope. These are:

> *"May the God of hope fill you with all joy and peace as you trust in him, so that you may overflow with hope by the power of the Holy Spirit."* (Rom 15:13)

> *"Be joyful in hope, patient in affliction, faithful in prayer."* (Rom 12:12)

It is my prayer that you may overflow with hope from the inspirational stories of these women. It is also my prayer that every reader will have hope for their eternal future.

> *"I pray that the eyes of your heart may be enlightened in order that you may know the hope to which he has called you, the riches of his glorious inheritance in his holy people."* (Eph 1:18)

Chapter 1

Samantha Leonoski

How Does Hope Bring Transformation?

My biological mother, Vonette Leonard, gave birth to me at Royal North Shore hospital in St Leonards, Sydney. It was a close call as I nearly arrived in the back of a combi van which at the time she was living in. She left me at the hospital claiming that she wasn't ready to have a child to raise and I spent my first two years being cared for by my Aunty Berris and Nana Esma.

After two years, my mum decided to collect me, punching my aunty in the face in the hallway, reefing me out of her arms and we were off to live a life of varied adventures. I did not know any different when I was a small child growing up in these circumstances, but it was a life of abuse of all kinds – homelessness and poverty. I learnt how to survive. My start to life was precarious and full of ways to overcome adversity.

I lived with my alcoholic biological mother until I was eight years old. I had four sisters, however, my eldest sister never lived with me at any stage of my life. She was left at the hospital and taken into my Nana's care. She had a serious skin disorder known commonly as a "cotton wool" baby. This proved too difficult for my mum who, at that time, was 23 years old.

I'm the second eldest of five girls. I was the eldest to my three younger sisters who I looked after as best I could – even though I was a child myself. We lived in the bush, refuges, squatted in abandoned houses until finally, we were eligible to move into a housing commission home in Byron Bay. It wasn't long after this time that a lot of the homeless people of Byron Bay would come and stay in our home.

My sister Olivia and I attended Byron Bay Primary School as much as we could. I loved school as it was where I could play all sorts of sport at lunch and escape the responsibilities of looking after my younger sisters. Olivia and I would go out to steal food for everyone and make cubby houses in the bush for a place to get away. I have memories of going to the back of *Woolworths* where they'd throw out their old produce and we'd get what we could. On other occasions, we'd walk into *Woolworths* and fill a trolley full of food and then walk straight out. No one ever stopped us and to my knowledge, never suspected us of stealing.

My mother was rich every fortnight from welfare payments that seemed to all go on alcohol. She turned into a nasty person and I would find myself standing up to her. I put salt and pepper in her *schooner* once at the main beach pub. She humiliated me and poured the beer all over me and made a big scene. I had to wash off in the surf and something in that moment changed for me.

In my mind, I was trying to stop her from drinking the poison that in turn would ruin our life. Mum was evidently kicked out of every pub in Byron Bay and knew the local constable all too well. There was a time where she stabbed me with a fork when I was trying to protect one of my sisters from another drunken beating. There were other times where she burnt the back of my hand with her cigarette butt. To this day, I have a constant reminder of hardship every time I see my burn scars – this can be very humbling during difficult times.

My mother was very paranoid about doctors so we would have a nurse visit our home to give us our immunisations and look in on my youngest two sisters who had complications. My sister SR was born brain damaged and with water on her brain. SR had surgery to implant a shunt to drain the water from her brain. She was constantly bashed by my mother to stop her crying. There was an episode where Mum threw her against the wall and then down the stairs. The final straw before SR was taken away into other permanent care was when she was raped at two years old and required surgery. Her rapist, who was a homeless junky, visited our housing commission home for shelter like many others. He ended up hanging himself in Grafton Jail. My youngest sister, Shana, had to wear leg braces as she was born with a turned in foot and required surgery to correct it.

One time, I was playing chase with Olivia and she was running after me and I stood behind the bedroom door waiting for the precise moment to slam the door in her face. And that's exactly what happened, however the doorknob hit her straight in the middle of her forehead giving her a massive lump. The lump receded and then two black eyes appeared on her face just before school photos. We did our best to try and hide them so we could still get photos, but it was suspected that something else untoward went on. I found this an opportunity for me to reveal what a turbulent environment we lived in, so I lied in an interview at school on that account. I said that Mum had hit her. Mum would never hit Olivia as she was her favourite. Olivia was the only child that didn't challenge her.

Not too much longer after this event the day came when my class was in the media room watching *Free Willy* and I was asked to go to the office where waiting for me was my ticket out of my current life with my mum.

While reflecting on who or what gave me hope for the future, there were many impactful individuals that God has put on my path who have given me hope and there have been crucial interactions for me to make certain choices. My sisters and I went through the court system and my mother even turned up for a session in Ballina where she stood up and proclaimed that she was raped by her brother-in-law growing up. She was told to sit down but continued to shout and was removed from the court.

This was the first time I witnessed my mum fight for us. It was too late. All three of us were put into the custody of my Aunty Berris (Aunty B), her husband (Uncle T) and my cousins in Toowoomba. This was a great time as I had boy cousins to play sport with, a huge yard, delicious meals and family time. Plus, I had a loving aunty and Nana who were so patient and kind.

How Does Hope Bring Transformation?

We went to church and I attended a Christian school (Christian Outreach College) where I respected my teachers as they seemed more caring and compassionate and somewhat different to what I'd known in my previous life. I also delved into reading. I couldn't get enough of books. I'd have up to five books on the go at once and would sit high up in a tree and would read for hours on end. I also discovered a side of me that investigated things in the world from a scientific view. I'd collect butterflies and insects and find out their scientific name. I found so much joy in knowledge. I just couldn't get enough information and I felt safe and supported in this learning. I dove deep into studying the Bible at this young age and began my relationship with God. All I wanted to do was to help other people and be the best person I could be. I was always positive which later I learnt can be a protective mechanism and you can slip into toxic positivity. I still needed to be able to deal with conflict which came much later in life.

I played soccer, basketball, tennis and did athletics, softball and cricket. I excelled in anything sport and had so many best friends. My sports teacher, Mrs Harch, had taught Kathy Freeman and saw great potential in me too. Her daughter, Lana, was one of my best friends. We played representative soccer and were great at running. Pastor Hands was my headmaster at the school I attended and he'd often give me tips and valuable pointers that I've hung onto my whole life. At my local church, Pastor Shelton was also someone I listened to and took advice on how to transform my life into something and into someone worthy of helping others.

Three years into this life, the beast of abuse raised its ugly head once again and my sister Olivia revealed that she'd been sexually abused by Uncle T. Subconsciously, I took this on as not being able to protect her and felt guilty for this for a good chunk of my life. And so off we were again to yet another home. My guard went back up.

Some foster parents were incredible and others were in it for the money. There was abuse and addiction all through this system. I learnt to protect my sisters as best I could. Not many families wanted us three girls together, but we did our best not to get separated as long as possible.

From the age of eight to 13 years, I was in and out of 13 different foster homes. My sisters and I never returned to my mother's care. My sisters and I were split up shortly after living with my Aunty B and her family for three years. There was and still is a shortage of foster carers so we had no chance of sticking together.

At 13, I was finally placed with a family in Byron Bay – or rather Suffolk Park. Sue White and Peter Emery were my new parents. Both ex-Navy, I was faced with a regimental way of living. This was a catalyst time for me and the beginning of something great. Structure and stability is what they offered and I thrived on that. They hadn't had children together and they really didn't want any more foster children, but the department was desperate and pleaded just to have me for the weekend.

That was the start of my new life. I walked in with a bit of a hardened attitude and stated that I wanted a dog, I only wore name brands and I didn't eat chocolate, I only ate carob. Sue and Peter stated that there were three rules: Don't steal, don't lie and the rest we'll make up as we go along.

That weekend we all grew to know one another more and they softened and so did I. To this day, I still call them Mum and Dad – although not directly but in reference. Although Dad sadly passed away peacefully in his sleep at the tender age of 59.

How Does Hope Bring Transformation?

From the support, encouragement and unconditional love I received from my new parents I decided that I could live out my dreams and in order to do this I had to start with small goals. I attended Byron Bay High School and I had a Maths and an English teacher that saw my potential and wouldn't let me just fly under the radar and not work towards my full capabilities. I continued to excel academically and more so in sport. I made the State and National teams for running and soccer. This gave me scope to gain a sports scholarship at a private school in Lismore called Trinity Catholic College. With my achievements, I told myself I'd focus on education, career and buying a home and having a family.

I made it into the shadow Australian Matilda's soccer team at the age of 15. A season later, I then discovered I had significant scoliosis. I had an S-shaped spine with 53 and 47 degrees curvature. The curves were so severe that surgery had to occur within a month. My future soccer dreams of representing the Matilda's were shattered.

At the age of 17, I had two Harrington rods inserted on the sides of my spine with bolts and screws to hold them in place. The rods were supposed to stay in for life. I even grew 3cm after the eight-hour surgery. I couldn't bend or twist and walked around with perfect posture.

After I graduated from school, I figured it best to get a career where I was able to retreat to a desk to be ergonomically correct with a combination of outside work to remain relatively active. The surgeon had suggested to always lead an active life as this gave me structural strength and integrity for my spine and had saved me from a more serious condition.

I was successful in gaining a traineeship with surveyors in Lismore. This position also allowed me to venture further into surveying for a council job. Three years after the surgery, I had a horrible infection throughout my spine and the rods were removed after three more surgeries to flush the infection.

I then set my intentions on property ownership. I worked three jobs to save for the purchase of my first home when I was 20. I met my first daughter's father at this time and had Lydia when I was 23. Lydia went to full time day-care at five weeks old so that I could continue to work full time and uphold the mortgage and keep our little piece of Australia. This occurred due to me securing a stable job.

Shortly afterwards, her father and I separated. We didn't have the same morals and values to raise a child together and I never wanted to become a statistic of a broken family, but conversely, I didn't want my daughter to endure an unhappy household.

It was revealed to me – ironically after a Pinktober Pedal 50km cycle ride for cancer – that I in fact had thyroid cancer. The director of my branch at council, Debra Howe, had been through her own ordeal with cancer and supported me having time to heal after treatment and surgery – along with offering her research of food recipes to combat cancerous cells and positive affirmations to assist with recovery and a healthy mindset.

Throughout this time, I then had another evaluation period of life during my sick leave and chose to apply to several universities for full time study in order to be a sports teacher. Coincidently, I chose the University of the Sunshine Coast to study a dual degree in Secondary Education and Science. I'd gained confidence and assurance that I was capable of university studies through all my support networks and I had faith I was able to succeed. Uni was tough at times and I met a few demons and anxiety blocks that I had to conquer in order to overcome and prevail. Constant self-reflection and having hope that God had my back got me through the many challenges.

During uni, I had a tutor that recognised and respected my papers I submitted for my teaching degree subjects and he encouraged me in my final year that doing a remote placement would be advantageous due to my life experiences. His name was Kenneth and he stated that I could either be a missionary or mercenary during my time in a remote community that had such little to no access to opportunities.

After four years of university studies, my daughter and I moved to Doomadgee due to me successfully acquiring a permanent teaching placement. During this turbulent yet exciting time, I learnt not to be narrow-minded and have an appreciation for the doors of opportunity to success that potentially opened up. I wanted to show initiative in areas of my life I felt compelled to travel towards. Insightfully and through mindfulness and meditation, I have proven to be quite the strategist to systematically have a goal to work towards constantly. If something changes along the way, it's on me and my ability to overcome a setback and create a renewed goal. Constant management of dealing with failing attempts enables me to be grateful for that opportunity overall. It's all about attitude.

Doomadgee was an experience next to none, but nothing surprised me. My daughter Lydia and I endured severe prejudice, and she was subjected to bullying and saw me when I had my wrist sprained by a student when I was trying to apprehend a weapon. Lydia witnessed a baby being delivered at the front gates of the school. One time on playground duty, I felt a cloud of dust rise as a crowd was running and a passing student informed me that they had

Lydia. I immediately went to the playground where my daughter had been cornered and rocks thrown at her calling her all the names under the sun. She was seven and didn't quite understand what was taking place. She was encouraged by other students to bash others in order to have friends. Lydia was even tripped over, held down and strangled during a cross country run.

Although these events occurred, we managed to stay there much longer than most and I was convinced to finally move when one of my fellow teachers had her horses set free and some mutilated and she was cornered and came very close to being raped. Other teachers had their car windows smashed and things taken.

Furthermore, students would make weapons like shanks, spears and slingshots and hide them in the gutters for easy access. Classrooms had to be locked and I still found myself years later in other schools ensuring doors are locked properly three times over. My saving grace was being invited by the Elder Aunties of the community to join them at church on Sundays. This is where I found myself enjoying cups of tea and listening to their voices bellowing the choruses of old tunes I'd remembered from visits to the Salvation Army with my Nana Esma when I was a child. It felt safe. I donated a great deal of clothes, gym equipment and even a trampoline to the community. I could sense these niceties were welcomed with open arms like I was to the church. I didn't know that this was a Brethren Church initially, and I was the first unmarried women to come to their church, so that was something I cherished.

When I moved from Doomadgee to Townsville for my next teaching placement, I decided to attend a church that was recommended by the Elders which was one they visited if they went to Townsville for health, school or family reasons. Here I connected with more people of like minds. I continued to meet more wonderous people

How Does Hope Bring Transformation?

in the Townsville community, including Amanda Nickson. It's amazing who is placed in your life at certain times and there are a select few in life who I've felt safe to reveal my past to. There have also been a couple of times where I have mistakenly told people I naively trusted and they have either run for the hills and never wanted to have anything else to do with me or expressed pity and labelled me incorrectly as unstable. Wanting to be accepted over the years, these responses have made me very cautious of what and who I tell my story to, as ignorance can breed fear. Another protective strategy of mine.

It is this time that I feel comfortable and have let down many walls to acknowledge that perhaps my story can do exactly what I've always wanted... To help others. Thanks to Amanda for planting the seed to share my story so many years ago. I've considered and started many times but to no deadline and would put it aside when times got busy. Fortunately, I've always kept diaries since before I was put into foster care and all throughout my life to date.

While in Townsville, and a year before my boomerang transfer back to the coast, my dad passed away. The night before, we'd spoken about the importance of putting family first and me being able to make his 60th birthday in the August. The next morning, I went for my usual trek up Castle Hill where I had one of the regular walkers say good morning and point at the stars and said it was some special alignment. At that moment, I thought how much Dad would appreciate that as he studied astronomy as one of his interests. I learnt later that it was that exact time that he died. It struck me that such a knowledgeable human can just be gone and I've always said I wished he'd written a book. He had helped me so much over the years in his own way. He had a way and always meant for the best. He believed that you can always better yourself no matter what background you come from. Mum supports this and says that an individual ultimately has the power to make their own choices.

A year later, I was transferred to a teaching role on the Gold Coast. It took a good amount of sacrifice and hard work and I was able to set up a home for my daughter and I. I joined a running and walking group called *Twin Towns Runners and Social Walkers* who I consider family. It's so very comforting to be surrounded by supportive and reliable people and in this club I found some more lifelong friendships.

While in this group, I met my now husband, Andrew Schostakowski. He is everything I've desired and more. My heart is truly his as there were sparks from the very first time I set eyes on him after a running meet at Tallebudgera Creek. It may sound cliché, but it was love at first sight. I had a sudden feeling that I would marry him. It felt so organic, and I was instantly filled with admiration for him as he loyally respected and showed compassion and love for me. We instantly started to build a foundation together. He is my rock and I'm safe. He always supports my need for betterment and continues to encourage me to follow my dreams. With his intelligence, he has taught me to think more critically and I've been able to manage situations of conflict with greater perspective and awareness – whereas in the past, I'd shut down and move on.

Andrew and I are now married and share a beautiful daughter, Evelyn. We decided to create a new surname by combining parts of both our surnames and to essentially start life afresh. Andrew and I are now Mr and Mrs Leonoski. We have been fortunate enough with God's grace and favour to endeavour in starting a new family tree. I'm currently on maternity leave from my teaching position on the Gold Coast. I'm now residing in Abu Dhabi due to Andrew's work.

How Does Hope Bring Transformation?

It is at this time where I'm blessed enough to be able to have time off to be a full-time mother. I never had this time with Lydia but that was a very different life back then. I'm so very grateful and appreciative of this most important and empowering time in our lives. This would never have been able to happen if I didn't make those initial sacrifices and worked hard and endured and conquered the many adversities along the way. God has always been there paving the way.

Looking back on my past now, it has been pivotal that I find myself victorious and not a victim of the system. I attest my victorious attitude to having faith in God's plan along with my many positive influences of which I only mentioned but a few. Additionally, my thirst to learn and listen to podcasts, read literature and conduct research to better myself in order to be the person worthy of this life and to help others know their own potential and worth.

My current goal is to begin postgraduate studies in a Doctor of Medicine here in Abu Dhabi at Khalifa University. In the meantime, I will continue to immerse myself in motherhood and be fully present in these precious moments with my baby daughter. Life is so very fleeting. It's what you do with it that counts.

I believe that in every adverse situation there's always hope and there's a reason why you need to endure hardships in your life – to build resilience and solidify your worth. Your story may very well help others someday.

Samantha's favourite scriptures:

*"I lift up my eyes to the mountains—where does my help come from?
2 My help comes from the Lord, the Maker of heaven and earth.*

*3 He will not let your foot slip—
he who watches over you will not slumber;
4 indeed, he who watches over Israel will neither slumber nor sleep.*

*5 The Lord watches over you—the Lord is your shade at your right hand;
6 the sun will not harm you by day, nor the moon by night.*

*7 The Lord will keep you from all harm—he will watch over your life;
8 the Lord will watch over your coming and going both now and forevermore."* (Psalm 121)

"6 Do not be anxious about anything, but in every situation, by prayer and petition, with thanksgiving, present your requests to God.

7 And the peace of God, which transcends all understanding, will guard your hearts and your minds in Christ Jesus."
(Philippians 4:6-7)

"But the fruit of the Spirit is love, joy, peace, forbearance, kindness, goodness, faithfulness, 23 gentleness and self-control. Against such things there is no law." (Galatians 5:22-23)

"I can do all this through him who gives me strength."
(Philippians 4:13)

Questions to consider:

1. Is there someone I could share my current struggle with who could help me and bring me hope?

2. Is there someone that sharing some of my own story with could encourage them and give them reason to hope?

Chapter 2

Karene Gravener

How He Will Make a Way Where There is No Way

I am the middle child of three sisters. Shona is 18 months older than me and I have a younger sister, Rachelle who is six years younger than me. I also have a half-brother, Greg. Before Dad met Mum, Dad was in a relationship and, as many reading this will know that back in the 60s, if a woman fell pregnant, you didn't talk about it. In fact, Dad didn't even know that he was a father to a boy until a 26-year-old man wanted to find his dad.

I was born nine weeks premature. My mum had a fall, landing heavily on her stomach and, in the days and weeks that followed, she started leaking fluid, due to a small tear in the membranes surrounding me. She did all the right things and tried to stay as healthy as possible. However, she went into premature labour. She had a difficult labour, as her body was not ready to give birth; this led to complications, and consequently, I was losing oxygen.

I was born on the 3rd of April 1975. I was very tiny, weighing two pounds and three ounces. I was placed in an incubator, interestingly however, there were no exceptional circumstances noted regarding my health, and I was able to go home around my original due date which was between the 4th and the 6th of June. Over the following months, it became apparent that I was not meeting my milestones, and at approximately one year of age, I was diagnosed with cerebral palsy. Although as a family, we will never really know at what point cerebral palsy affected me and whether it was due to my mother's accident, or the birthing process, it is a part of me now.

I want to honour and thank my entire family. Mum and Dad are good, solid people who have always done the best they could with the resources and energy they had. My sisters mean the world to me, and we are all very close. It's amazing what you can see as an adult, and in retrospect. I want to acknowledge and give thanks to my sisters because I see with clarity that there were many times my sisters had to put their needs second to mine. That would not have been easy – especially when they too were young and had needs of their own.

I have always been extra close to my mum; I love her so much. She has been my rock and my encourager, and the one that pushed me to aim higher and dream bigger – even though for many years I couldn't see that. I was like any other kid, who saw her as a very annoying parent at times. I would always get frustrated when she would expect me to do my exercises or challenge me to do things that were good for my mobility and strength. I understand now that

How He Will Make a Way Where There is No Way

Mum was not just looking at today, but she was looking beyond to the future, and wanted me to achieve in life.

I believe Mum could see what I couldn't see, and that is like God's heart towards us – he can see in us what we may not see. Mum is someone who I have the utmost respect for. She is a woman who doesn't expect praise and has done her job as a mother because that's what she had to do. She doesn't understand the power of what she's done.

It wasn't until I was around 30 years old that I was able to sincerely apologize for being so difficult when I was younger. I had a lot of anger inside because of all the things that I couldn't understand. Growing up, I couldn't get my head around why I had to be 'different' or why I had to miss out on what other kids did. Nor could I understand why kids bullied me and left me out. I had a lot of sadness and anxiety, and I couldn't express the emotions and thoughts storming around inside of me. Sadly, Mum bore the brunt of all this. Children often think their parents are indestructible and that somehow their feelings don't matter. I now realize as a parent myself that the very opposite is true.

My Aunty Lorraine, Mum's older sister is also someone who I want to extend my deepest gratitude. From approximately one to six years of age, once a year, she would assist with the finances to allow me and Mum to travel to the Royal Children's Hospital in Sydney. Here, I would receive intensive physiotherapy, occupational therapy, and speech therapy for around two weeks at a time. Then, Mum would take these therapies and techniques back to Ayr where we lived and work on what we had learned. These therapies were extremely important for my development because there were many things I could not do, such as sit up independently, turn my head, lift my head, roll, crawl. Really, all the usual milestones were very difficult, and it took a lot of practice, continuous energy, and perseverance to learn so many things.

Today, Mum and I often reflect on Lorraine's goodness and generosity. We both see how her kindness and giving nature has been woven throughout the lives of our whole family and this has made our lives so rich. Without the blessing of being able to access such high-quality therapies, would I be the person I am today and would Mum have had the knowledge and understanding that she did?

My success was always at the forefront of my family's mind. As mentioned, I did occupational therapy, physiotherapy and speech therapy, but I also went horseback riding to improve my balance and to speech and drama lessons to improve my speech. Everything was done to help me achieve and grow. What is even more humbling for me to remember as an adult is that we were not always comfortable with finances. In fact, it was a struggle and yet, Mum and Dad always did everything they could to put their children first.

My dad is a straightforward and hardworking man. I believe that Dad would have done anything to be able to change what was and help me to walk. I have a vivid memory of being around 12 years of age, and Dad and I were talking before I went to sleep. Things must have been weighing heavily on his mind, because, seemingly out of nowhere he said to me, *"If I could give you my legs, I would."*

I remember being taken aback by this statement, not because it made me uncomfortable, but because it spoke volumes to me. Dad wanted to fix something, to make it right and he couldn't, and that made him sad. I remember to this day what my response was – with a sincere heart I said, *"I'm okay Dad. God knows what he is doing."*

How He Will Make a Way Where There is No Way

If I am being honest, it is fair to say that the relationship between Dad and I has not always been easy. Again, as an adult, I can see that Dad wanted the best for me. Consequently, he was strict and tough on me because he wanted me to be able to 'manage' and be independent. What I saw as him being unkind and mean was in fact him being overwhelmed about me not being okay and able to look after myself in life.

In 2002, God challenged me to write a letter to my father. At first, I couldn't understand why, but through a lot of prayer and reflection, I began to see that I needed to see Dad as a person first and then a father. I wrote a letter. Through writing this letter, I felt so much healing in my heart. It was a letter of forgiveness. A letter, which he still reads today. Mum often catches him reading it.

There is power in the written word. When things are written down, they keep giving life and hope. I feel like Dad reads that letter and feels like he is loved because I felt God's love through writing it.

My Faith Journey

Seeds of hope and faith have been planted in my heart and mind from a very young age. My mum helped me see a future for myself and encouraged me to do more than I thought I could in terms of physical abilities. She was always planting seeds in my mind and helping me to see that I could do things that I wanted to do. In the eyes of my family, I was no different; I was one of three children and was always told, *"If you set your mind to something, you will do it."*

I was with my first partner, Tony, when I was 19. We had been dating for about six months to a year and he said if we were to continue in our relationship, I needed to know God personally; to have a relationship with him. At the time, I certainly didn't like this being imposed on me, and took great offense to this ultimatum. However, of course God had other plans, and in his own way, he was leading me closer to him. I came to realise over the coming weeks, that being a Christian was not about doing it because other people were, it was because God loved me and had a plan and purpose for my life.

It was on the 8th of May 1997, in Ayr North Queensland where I came to know the power and the presence of Jesus Christ in my life, and where I came to understand the power of deliberately making a declaration of accepting Him as my Lord and Saviour and choosing to live for him all the days of my life. I remember as soon as this happened, a tangible power consumed my heart and my mind. I'll never forget that feeling.

Coincidentally, Dale, my husband, on the same weekend, attended the same crusade in Townsville the night before, and he received salvation. Who would have thought, that even then God had a part of us coming together? It wouldn't be until exactly nine years later that we would meet and discover this fact.

As is the experience of many young Christians, I began to ask God what wanted me to do with my life. I had always known I loved people and wanted to help them, but I was so unsure as to how to get there. Realistically, I asked and prayed for a long time; I remember being so certain that a way would be made for me to study Christian counselling at a Christian University, however as hard as I tried, the doors literally remained shut for me.

In time, I came to understand that my purpose was to be a light in the darkness and salt of the Earth and the path I was to take was a Bachelor of Social Work through James Cook University.

How He Will Make a Way Where There is No Way

Getting to university was a two-year journey. The biggest challenge was setting myself up with accommodation that was wheelchair accessible and personal care. I knew I had to plan meticulously and seek solutions for all the scenarios – both potential and real – that I would face as a young woman with a disability heading off to a new environment one hour away from home.

This process was not easy, as so many things did not exist for people with disabilities. There was no such thing as a university that provided on-site personal care, I didn't know where there would be any kind of accommodation that would be suitable for me, and certainly, I'd never lived away from home, so this whole idea was so far beyond what I could achieve on my own. I had to trust beyond what I'd ever trusted before and see with my heart what I could not yet see with my natural eyes.

> *"Now faith is the substance of things hoped for, the evidence of things not yet seen."* (Heb 11:1)

This was not always easy; it would be foolish to say so. There were times when I was so afraid and overwhelmed. In my heart, I knew I needed a word from God. I needed him to speak to my heart so that, come what may, I could rely on his promise for me. God, in his faithfulness did exactly that through Isaiah 43:

> *"Do not be afraid, for I have ransomed you. I have called you by name; you are mine. When you go through deep waters, I will be with you. When you go through rivers of difficulty, you will not drown. When you walk through the fire of oppression, you will not be burned up; the flames will not consume you. For I am the LORD, your God."*

This word, this living word literally leapt off the page into my heart and from that time it became life to me, and I had a peace that was unshakable. I know now, especially when I look back, that God knew I would need this for what was to come.

One of the strongest memories I have of God first providing and making a way, was through setting up a stakeholders meeting with the head of nursing, the disability liaison officer of James Cook University and a representative from independent advocacy in Townsville. Through honest conversations and collaboration, it was agreed that the head of nursing would allow first year nursing students to be a part of a volunteer roster to help with my personal care while waiting on funding from the government.

To this day, I still have friendships with some of those nursing students, and I know it wasn't just me being helped by these amazing women, it was a two-way street. I can't help but look back and see God's goodness. I had the privilege of living this scripture:

> *"And are confident that you yourself are a guide to the blind, a light to those who are in darkness."* (Rom 2:19)

I know that *"His strength was made perfect in my weaknesses."* (2 Corinthians 12:9)

In July 1998, in the wee hours of a Monday morning, this journey began. I remember driving up to Townsville with Mum, feeling so many emotions: fear, excitement, sadness and hope all in one. I was about to become a student at John Flynn College, James Cook University. Mum stayed the night with me, and I remember how she left early the next morning. It was not easy for her; in fact, I would later learn that she told a close friend she felt like she was *"losing her left arm."*

How He Will Make a Way Where There is No Way

She was so brave though, and I was brave too, to be honest. It was the first day of 'O-Week' and there were so many thoughts spinning around in my head, I didn't have time to think about my emotions and I literally hit the ground running.

In all honesty, the first semester of my degree was a very big blur. I failed the first two subjects that I attempted. All my energy was in survival mode. Yes, I had the volunteer roster with first year nursing students, and I also had a small amount of support from Blue Care Townsville, apart from that though, there were no other established supports for me at this stage, and so each day was literally a step of faith. I lost count of the number of times I would say *"God, who will I ask to help me today?"* or how many times I prayed:

> *"God is our refuge and strength, an ever-present help in trouble."* (Psalm 46:1)

As time went on, resources floated in a little bit more. I never stopped advocating for myself; it was a weekly commitment. I was determined to see my needs met so that I could focus on my purpose, and the reason why God had brought me to Townsville. People would often say to me, *"When you write your funding applications, just write it like you can't do anything, just paint your worst possible scenario to them."* – "them" being state and federal funding bodies.

Many times, the thought did cross my mind to do just that, but when it came down to it, I just couldn't do it. I wasn't going to portray myself as hopeless because I wasn't and I'm not. I refused to paint myself as unable. A funny example of this was when I told my story of self-advocacy to the Townsville Bulletin. They wanted a photo of me, and of course, I wanted to look my best, So, I had all my jewellery on, and my hair was perfect, and I'd picked my very best outfit. My sister was on the phone to me soon after the article was published, and she said jokingly, *"You're supposed to look desperate!"*

I replied, *"No way! I am who I am."*

I am so grateful for John Flynn College and the amazing community that it was for me. The college principal, Gary, is a beautiful Christian man. He was very good to me, and always did whatever he could to provide what I needed to function successfully within the college, and all the staff members and students were supportive and inclusive of me too. I often reflect on my time there and feel that a lot of hurt that was a part my school years was mended in those unforgettable experiences.

I graduated with a social work degree in April 2005, just five days after my 30th birthday. I will never forget how proud I felt walking across the stage to receive my bachelor's degree certificate. It was a wonderful night and so many family members travelled from everywhere to celebrate this momentous occasion with me.

In my time as a professional, I have worked in various environments, and I can see how my journey and my story have influenced the way that I support others. I always see someone's struggle as significant and real, but only a small part of their story and their future potential. I have also had many opportunities to participate in community events, conferences, and forums where I have shared my story and advocated for others passionately.

One forum that comes to mind revolved around the National Disability Insurance Scheme, it was 2013 and the scheme was in its early days. Many people with disabilities, and organisations representing people with disabilities were working tirelessly to ensure that this scheme was a success and developed in such a way that it be sustainable and accessible for the thousands of people who needed daily support for the rest of their lives. I was asked by the then Senator Jan McLucas' to present my story.

It was a very emotional experience for me. I desperately wanted people understand the isolation, sadness, despair and fear that people with disabilities experience when they don't have the support and resources they need to survive and function in a daily capacity. It was difficult for me to adequately express what it is like to feel like you are part of the world but not really part of the world because your basic human rights are not being met. I remember when I was sharing my story, I was doing it for myself, and the thousands of other individuals just like me.

I shared with the audience that living with a disability was like living in apartheid and how apartheid is a symbol of separation, of being less than – of having less rights, less access, less freedom, and very limited choice. I wanted the audience to understand that this story, my story was the story of thousands of people with disabilities for far too long, and that it was time for our voices to be heard.

Today in 2024, although the National Disability Insurance Scheme is established in Australia, I still I feel like I am fighting for change. My hope for the future is that the NDIS will grow stronger and become more inclusive, and that people with disabilities will come out of the shadows and into the light and into their potential. I want people with disabilities to be seen as people with hopes, dreams, aspirations, careers, lives, families, relationships, wants and needs because that's who and what we are!

I met my husband, Dale in 2006, and we got married on the 25th of July 2009. This date was deliberately chosen. We chose July because it is the month of my mother's birthday, we chose the 25th day to get married because the number five represents God's grace over our lives, and finally because July is the seventh month of the year, and seven represents God's perfect completion.

We have also been blessed with two beautiful children, Samuel, who was born on the 11th of August 2010, and Tori, who was born on the 6th of February 2016. I often tell them that they are my greatest achievement because they are!

Recently, I launched my online counselling business, *Karene Gravener Counselling Services*. I am excited about how this business will develop and the people that I will help. I genuinely feel that my experience both as a person and a professional will go a long way in inspiring and equipping others to stand strong and hold onto hope, even when things don't look hopeful.

When I reflect on my life, a song comes to mind that was popular about 20 years ago. In that song the chorus says, *"He will make a way where there is no way."*

That's how I feel about my life and how far I have come. Honestly, if you look with your natural eyes and consider all the facts and circumstances about my life, maybe you would be left with not much hope; but if you look through the eyes of faith, His truth remains and that is *"all things are possible for those who believe."* (Mark 9:23)

How He Will Make a Way Where There is No Way

Karene's favourite scriptures:

*"But now, this is what the Lord says—
he who created you, Jacob,
he who formed you, Israel: 'Do not fear, for I have redeemed you; I have summoned you by name; you are mine. When you pass through the waters, I will be with you; and when you pass through the rivers, they will not sweep over you.
When you walk through the fire,
you will not be burned; the flames will not set you ablaze.
For I am the Lord your God,
the Holy One of Israel, your Saviour.'"* (Isaiah 43:1-3)

Questions to consider:

1. Having determination to find a way to live independently and to study when there seemed to be no way to do it was Karene's strength. What situation do you need to be determined about finding a way forward?

2. Are there circumstances you could advocate for, either in your own life or for someone else? How could you do that effectively? What is the first step?

Chapter 3

Julie Mengel

How Does Hope Bring Dreams and Possibilities to Life?

As it is with many people, I have had some big challenges in my life with my upbringing and early family life and later, as a single parent with some serious health challenges.

I was the eldest of three girls. My mum and dad divorced when I was 19 after many years of arguments and tension. I knew Dad was having affairs as I found many love letters that a woman had written to Dad and I gave them to Mum. I don't know what I was thinking at the time as I was probably around 11 or 12. However, they began attending marriage guidance counselling and I had to go with them because I gave Mum the letters.

Looking back, I can't believe how inappropriate that was on so many levels. Not only for my parents allowing it but the questionable ethics of the counsellor at the time. They stayed together until I was 19, however, the writing was on the wall for a long time.

My father was a family man who loved his family, but he was a drinker who was gregarious and trusted everyone. He would bring hitchhikers home for dinner. He had no filter. They would be people he didn't know and although he offered them hospitality, for three young girls, it was dangerous.

I can vividly remember being molested in our lounge room when everyone went outside one day, I might have been 11 or 12. When I told Dad about it, he said, *"You must be imagining things!"*

When my uncle was doing the same thing to children, he was in denial. Dad said, *"Julie, that would never happen, you know you're a creative girl with a vivid imagination, you don't know what you're talking about."*

It was not until many years later that I realised the extent of the co-dependency and the many other issues that we were all living through. I didn't see a lot of affection between my parents. I really think there was much damage done as this was my role model for family and marriage. I thought to myself, *"I'm never getting married."*

There was also the guilt of when they'd argue, I would think, *"Why don't you just get a divorce?"*

When they did, I thought I had caused it. As the eldest, I took on much of the responsibility and strived to be the peacemaker.

How Does Hope Bring Dreams and Possibilities to Life?

My early family life had a real effect on my relationships. I didn't have any rules to go by and no moral guidelines, no boundaries. I didn't know I could say no to anything as my default was to keep everybody happy. However, I have always known there was something bigger than me. I remember talking to God around the age of nine and asking Him to be with me and come into my heart.

At 19, I went to live with my aunt and uncle in Sydney and began working at *Qantas* as my uncle worked there. Travel was exciting and staff would only have to pay 10% for flights. I went to Brazil for $40! On a trip to Fiji for four days, I met a woman swimming at Beachcomber Island who was a Canadian. She stayed at my place for a couple of months, and we became firm friends. I then flew to Vancouver for $30. I had a great time traveling around. I didn't know she had a Christian faith. Once we realised we both did, it deepened our friendship and opened a new realm. Her mother and her friends were Christian, too.

I moved to Townsville in 1983 after two years working on Dunk Island. I had decided I couldn't ignore my desire to study art any longer as I had always drawn and written poetry. I applied at a few universities and chose to stay in Townsville and complete my art degree.

My daughter was born in 1987 as I was finishing university, and my son was born in 1993. We started going to Sun City Christian Church in Townsville when my son was nearly three years old in 1996. At this stage, I was a single parent and many of the men in the church were wonderful role models for my children. This was a great support for me.

I was teaching full time at the Townsville Grammar School and had taken a group of 20 students on a trip to Italy for history and art. We were walking around 10,000 steps a day on our tour and unbeknownst to me at the time, I had contracted dengue fever. I remember I felt so ill in Venice I couldn't keep walking. I went to the hospital there and they thought it was mad cow disease. They really had no knowledge of tropical diseases. Upon my return to Townsville after a harrowing flight home, my body went into a state of chronic fatigue and I had to have a term off work to recover.

The irony was that I was the first aid woman for this trip. The first day after travelling to Italy, I was so fatigued, I remember asking myself, *"What's wrong with me?"*

I just felt like sleeping and I had to keep walking and walking. I was telling myself repeatedly to *"Get it together."*

I just had to keep going and going. I didn't know I had dengue fever until I was back in Townsville. At the doctor's surgery, I was so exhausted I couldn't even sit up and I was laying on the floor. That's when I was told, *"You've got full blown dengue."*

They said there is no way you could have been walking all over Italy, kilometres a day – but I did. I know God sustained me and carried me through it.

Not long after, I developed more health problems. I'd gone to stay with some friends on Magnetic Island for a few days and the doctor had diagnosed me with fibromyalgia. My body was so exhausted, I couldn't get up but I had to get back to work. As a single parent, I had no option but to push myself. I was the Aussie battler with the mortgage. It was like my body was breaking down and I just had to keep going.

Health is a big thing as a single parent because if the enemy wants to attack a single mum, it will be in health, money and their children.

How Does Hope Bring Dreams and Possibilities to Life?

I think there were so many times when God carried me through. I was so burned out but had to go on and I think sometimes you get to that point just before a breakthrough where everything seems to intensify.

There was another major health challenge not long after when I collapsed at work with diverticulitis. Throughout that year, I was hospitalised seven times which involved nil by mouth and strong intravenous antibiotics. I lost around 11kg during that time. By that Christmas, my sister and I were holidaying at Coolum on the Sunshine Coast when my bowel ruptured in the middle of one of the fiercest storms I had ever experienced on the coast. Needless to say, I felt the ambulance going over every pothole in the pouring rain as they tried repeatedly to cannulate me. I think it was by the grace of God that I made it to the hospital.

After two weeks in hospital on the coast with more antibiotics to reduce the infection, I desperately needed surgery and one of the best bowel specialists had moved me to the top of the list. Of course, at the same time, Cyclone Yasi was due to hit the Townsville area and my surgery was cancelled. I had to stay on strong antibiotics for six weeks while I waited for the surgery. My hair was falling out and my body felt as if it was being destroyed by all the strong drugs.

Throughout the many hospital visits, I made a list of Bible scriptures that I would pray over daily and it carried me through many difficult moments as I relied on the promises of God. I would meditate on each word, breaking it down. If I read the story of Esther, I became Esther and imagined her experiences as I was reading. God was providing the spiritual nourishment I needed at the time, and it strengthened my faith immeasurably. I finally had the surgery and some complications followed.

> *"Not only so, but we also glory in our sufferings, because we know that suffering produces perseverance; perseverance, character; and character, hope. And hope does not put us to shame, because God's love has been poured out into our hearts through the Holy Spirit, who has been given to us."*
> (Rom 5:3-5)

I had many weeks lying in a hospital bed over that time and I decided to create a list of my heart's desires. I wanted to stop working; to move to the Sunshine Coast; (we had been going down there every Christmas holiday for years) to be healthy and to do my artwork.

I had been reading that passage in the Bible:

> *"Take delight in the Lord, and he will give you the desires of your heart."* (Ps 37:4)

I thought about what I really wanted. I didn't want to keep working at this pace and God answered all the desires of my heart.

Everything on my list has happened! I met Baz at the end of 2010. We dated for two years and I resigned from my teaching position in Townsville and sold my house. We married in 2013 (after 22 years as a single parent) and I moved to the Sunshine Coast. My husband has built me a wonderful art studio in the bush near our creek and I am now able to do art full time.

I have had a yearning for a long time to create artwork that reflects the power of God. That seeing my work, people will be led to Him. This year I am undertaking a prophetic training course and I'm writing down words that inspire me from the course that I will develop into a visual format. It might be a word of faith and I'll try and visualise something.

How Does Hope Bring Dreams and Possibilities to Life?

I don't think I've reached my full creative potential yet; He has put a burning desire in me to do more. I have done some commissioned paintings and have had numerous exhibitions over the years, but I feel that I am not going into the depths that God wants me to go to. I want to go deeper.

What has given me hope in difficult times has been my Christian faith and my dear friends. My belief in God has been one of the hardest things in artistic circles – for me to name God as my inspiration, when a lot of other artists believe the opposite.

Another thing that really boosted my faith and took my mind away from my issues in earlier years was when a woman from church and I got together each week to feed and chat to the Aboriginal people who were living under the bridge in town. We did this for about a year and I would make a large pot of soup and go there with Sasha and my children. The people were so loving and welcoming.

One night, a group of young guys went past and threw broken bottles at everybody. The men we were chatting with stood up and stood over my children to protect them. I was amazed that the men were so protective of my children.

More recently, we have a team at our church that are praying and visiting anyone that needs encouragement. I am hoping to visit those in hospital as I know what it is like to wait for healing.

Having close friends have been a wonderful blessing in my life as well as other believers, like my Canadian friend. Quite often, we call each other and pray. She has been a real constant in my life, as was her mum. Her mum was a little woman who was one of the biggest prayer warriors I've ever met in my life. She had been praying for a good man for me for 20 years. Then I met my husband, and she was so happy to see that I had met someone like Baz.

My grandmother was another blessing to me, and I only found out that she was a praying Christian later in life. We would always call each other every Sunday; however, she didn't know I was praying and I didn't know she was praying. She lived 100 years and she was a strong, loving Christian matriarch to her family. In church one Sunday, God told me he has prepared His throne room for my grandmother. I didn't know God had a throne room at that time, so I knew it must have been God!

My hope for the future now is to create more of my artwork and saying yes when opportunities come up. I keep reflecting on the poem about the footprints in the sand*. I've always said for me, it is just the one set of footprints where God was carrying me, but I'm sure there is a drag mark where God has just been dragging me along, or pulling me out of the hole I was in.

I see the future getting better and better because I'm praying for my family and extended family constantly; that it's just a matter of time before they are going to get their breakthrough.

In church now we have a growing youth group. It's wonderful to see young people who have come in with their stories and hardships and see them begin to flourish.

I'm excited for the future with the joy of being a grandparent and having a great church family. The future is bright.

---

* https://footprintssandpoem.com/mary-stevenson-version-of-footprints-in-the-sand/

How Does Hope Bring Dreams and Possibilities to Life?

Julie's favourite scriptures:

"Trust in the Lord with all your heart and lean not on your own understanding; In all your ways acknowledge Him, And He shall direct your paths." (Prov 3:5-6, NKJV)

"Do not store up for yourselves treasures on earth, where moths and vermin destroy, and where thieves break in and steal. But store up for yourselves treasures in heaven, where moths and vermin do not destroy, and where thieves do not break in and steal. For where your treasure is, there your heart will be also." (Matt 6:19-21, NIV)

Questions to consider:

1. Julie was determined to follow her passion of art despite the challenges of being a single parent. What are you passionate to pursue despite obstacles?

2. When Julie was struggling with health challenges, she found some key scriptures to remind her that with God all things are possible. What key scriptures can be your anchors to faith and hope for the future?

Chapter 4

Sharon Henderson

How Does Relying on God Bring Hope?

I was eight years old when I went to a church, and I met Jesus. Since then, I'm now 55 and there has never been anybody else who can get me out of the hopelessness I've known. In any problem, my faith is what has made life possible.

I grew up in poverty in Papua New Guinea. There was one parent working to provide food for his own children, and then extended families coming in. My father would be going without. My parents were part of the United Church. I didn't feel any different or any closeness to God at that church. It was just like going for the sake of my parents making me go.

Until one day, this vehicle drove past with this flag flying with the slogan:

"One way, Jesus."

I saw that sign and I started running after it. It led me to where there were a few white missionaries; Canadians and Australians. They invited me in, and I went in. That's when I became interested in Jesus, just hearing about him feeding the people with five loaves and two fish. That's when I gave my heart to the Lord. I wanted this Jesus because they said there was only one way to heaven. That is true, Jesus Christ – He is the way, the truth and the life. I wanted this because I wanted happiness.

After that meeting, I took my brothers and sisters there. There were six of us. I was the eldest of the six. This got me into a lot of trouble and a lot of beatings by my mum because of my choice to follow the Assemblies of God movement, a different church to where my parents went. Later in life, any time I moved, I found a church that was affiliated with the Assemblies of God.

I met my husband in PNG when he was working for the bank over there and I was in hospitality. He was an Englishman. We both moved to England, got married in 1984 and moved to Australia. He was the kindest and most generous man and was very good to my family. I had not had any children with my husband but we were happily married. In 1990, I went back to Papua New Guinea, because my dad was very ill. That's where my life dramatically changed.

I met a man who was married in PNG when I visited my father. He was my brother's boss and he wanted me to be with him. I told him I was a happily married woman. I had my rings on and made this clear. He got some old man to use 'black magic' on me, which I had heard about but had not experienced before.

That night, I had a meal with my family and my brother and his friends, including this man, and after that meal, I started having feelings and thoughts for that man. The next day, I was supposed to fly back to Australia, but instead, I stayed in PNG with him. He is now the father of my children.

I stayed in PNG with him. The beatings started the week that I met him. It was a life that I had never experienced before. He was beating me every day and was a womaniser.

We decided to come back to Australia in 1996. We had four children when we came here again – they were five, three and two years old and the youngest was just two months old. I stayed with him, and we had seven children in total. He left us in 2009 when he went to prison for misappropriating money.

With heavy steps I got myself into church again. I started life alone with my children. I worried that people would judge me for being a single mother of many children and I did not want to say my husband was in prison. He hadn't allowed me to work. He said, *"Your duty is the home."* He was an accountant and an auditor and was able to provide for the household. That's when I realised that even though I had a relationship with God, I didn't previously have to rely on God because I had everything that I needed.

Once I was by myself, I started to depend on God. I was ashamed. What was I going to do? Who was going to provide for my children? To this day, I still hold onto God because I look at myself – I was in that pit, that dark place of despair. God reached in and he took me out. And he said *"Why are you looking at a man who would only be there for a short time?"*

I know there's no other way but God. Only God, not men, will give you all that you need.

That year, 2009, was when I realised how Australia is a blessed country and how blessed I was to live here. I say it's the *"Land of milk and honey"* because the government blesses the citizens and its residents to provide for them. That was my way I looked at it as God's provision for me – with provision from the government. I budgeted well and I took care of my children. And then I encouraged them to find part-time work after school, and we all worked together to support the family. It was not easy, but we were able to overcome.

I'm grateful to be in Australia, living here for my children's education. Three of my children were born here. They all grew up here. Education is everything. And the life that they have now, I am grateful to God for that. Because in Papua New Guinea, I would be suffering because there is not the support for a single parent. I am grateful to God, who gave me a new country to make my home and to raise my children in.

My youngest child, Josh, was born in 2007. He has multiple disabilities, and that has not been easy. As he is getting older, his behaviours are more challenging at times and it has been more difficult for me to manage. I am on my knees every day and night in my house, asking God to give me the strength to go on, because *"You gave Josh to me, and you have a purpose and a reason"*.

I accept responsibility for my son, no matter what happens. I wouldn't trade him for another person. Because he makes me know who God is. The pain of hopelessness, of not knowing what to do, because with his disabilities and his behaviours, it can happen anytime, without any warning. I don't know what's going to happen this afternoon or tomorrow.

Recently he was diagnosed with Level Two Autism on top of ADHD, a hearing impairment and an intellectual disability. He also had epilepsy and was incontinent, but in 2019, God healed him of the epilepsy and the incontinence. He was in nappies until 2019. That is when I cried out to God and I said, *"It is a miracle that my son is 13 but culturally, I can't touch my son (to help him use the toilet) as he has become a young man. God help me."*

And He got him out of the nappies. Josh went to toilet and the epilepsy stopped. Those two ailments were removed from his disabilities.

When I had Josh, I was in hospital for 15 days. My blood pressure was 225 over 125 and I was fighting for my life with it. And Joshy was on life support, fighting for his life. Josh's father never visited me when I was in the women's hospital. I had to ring his lover up and say, *"Can you please ask him to come and see me?"*

It took her to make my husband come in. When he arrived, he said, *"What do you want?"*

I replied, *"Who am I to you?"*

"Because of you my son is born that way," he answered.

The hospital had countless people come and talk to me because of Josh's situation. I prayed every night. That's all I did was when he was on the life support. I stepped into the corner of the room, and I cried out to God. I said, *"Lord, but the doctor said if he survives, he'll be a vegetable. He will not walk or talk or anything. No. He's my second son – I am willing to be his mother. Every day is the battle for him. Lord, you gave him to me for a reason."*

Because one thing is I had more patience. I had no patience at all before having Josh. But I needed patience.

I have spinal injuries and have had major surgery on my L1 and L2. I believe it was damage from being kicked in the back by my husband. He also lifted me up and had thrown me down on the ground. He would physically abuse me every week. I had surgery on my spine, but it didn't work as expected. I am supposed to have more surgery on my L3 as well, but I refused it because if it didn't help me the first time, why should I have it? I believe in a miracle working God.

I'm going to let God heal me in his time. When I didn't have this pain, I was responsible. But now every minute, every hour, I'm thanking God that I'm still breathing and have a life where others do not. I'm still able to walk – thank you for the pain because it makes me talk to you all the time. Well, I wouldn't change my life now for another. I wouldn't want it, because right now it's a life dependent on and holding on to Him.

When people talk about domestic violence, I know what it's like. There was one time he knocked me out. I was unconscious. I saw myself with the clouds and I saw myself lying down. I was walking to this bright light. He was calling me – it seemed very far away. He lifted me into the bath and filled it with water and ice. I was trying to get back and get up because the children were crying and when I came back and woke up, I was in a bath. He beat me even during pregnancy all the way up to birth.

How Does Relying on God Bring Hope?

My husband never went to prison for anything with the domestic violence. I never followed through on any charges because my children would cry. They would say, *"But ... he will go to jail. Then who's going to look after us?"* Police would come to the house, and I would have swollen and black eyes - my eyes were shut. There would be blood on my face, and I couldn't even see, and I would tell them *"I instigated it. I don't want to press charges."* This happened many times when I lived in Lismore. I would withdraw an order about domestic violence on him. I was in survival mode, and I depended on him. He had me believing that I couldn't survive without him.

I found out I could survive. It was all lies. After, when I was on my own, I saw that God already gave me a government that could help its citizens. My children are all working good jobs now – except Josh who is still in school. I have seven, beautiful children. I never regret telling my kids that they are a gift from God. When I look at it, I think to myself, *"God, did I really raise them? I am so proud of them."*

God gave me a child with disabilities because I had no patience in my life. When I asked him, *"Why can't you give me patience? I can't take this. I've lost it."*

God said, *"I gave you Joshua for you to have patience."*

That's where you learn how to be patient. I've now learned to be patient, to humble myself and to take things one day at a time. I cannot live without God. I need to tap into Him – I need this and I need Your ideas. Not my ideas, but Your ideas, Your way. I pray, *"Jesus, you increase, and I decrease. I breathe you in and I breathe myself out."*

Every day, I pray this way.

When my husband was in prison, I was visited by a woman who would bring Christmas gifts to the families of prisoners. She came to the house and asked, *"Have you got seven kids?"* and I nodded.

"We're from the prison. Your husband told us to come and see you. We just want the ages of your children, so we can buy some Christmas presents for them."

They came back with gifts for the children. I was very grateful.

These same people involved in the prison ministry asked me whether I would like to be involved with Kairos Prison Ministry for women in North Queensland. I went away as a guest to see what they did. I was so touched with these ladies from all different denominations serving women on a retreat in Kennedy. At the end, they performed a ceremony. It was very moving.

I was invited a second time and I connected very well with the Aboriginal and Torres Strait Islander women. They were sitting separate from everyone else, and I went and connected with them and encouraged them to be involved. I explained I'm from Papua New Guinea and that *"even though the people in charge are white, it doesn't matter what our skin colour is, because our blood is the same. We are red blood relatives – we all have red blood."*

I loved talking to the Indigenous woman there. They began to feel that they were good enough. I always reminded them that they were good enough.

This ministry was in June every year. I went for a few years from about 2014-2017. I wasn't involved so much for myself, even though my children's father was in prison. I felt that it was where I could relate to others because of the life we shared without husbands or

How Does Relying on God Bring Hope?

with family members in prison. As Josh got older and had more behaviour challenges, I felt I couldn't go away and be involved in this ministry anymore. My first responsibility was and is to my family.

My hope for the future is for my children to come back into the house of God to worship. They're not in the church. I want them to know what Jesus did for them. I want to leave a legacy that my grandchildren will see God and love the Lord. I hope they see with me, despite what I went through, that I held onto God. That's my hope for my children and my grandchildren.

Before my back injury, the life that I lived was all about sport. I was a state player for netball in Western Australia. I would go to church with my sports uniforms in my bag and would sit there, looking at the time while I listened to the preacher. And I'd leave church even if it was still going to get to my netball games. It now reminds me of how good and loving God is.

My hope now is to be an inspiration to somebody else, or a role model to somebody. I have lived as a single mother for 15 years now. I look at my daughters, and I try to be a good role model for them. If God wants me to have a companion, He will provide, but right now, I'm not searching for that.

I love my grandchildren – one girl and three boys. I call them my moon and stars. Briella is my moon and the boys are my stars. In my darkest times, when I'm down, as soon as they walk through the door, they shout, *"Bu Bu!"*

That's what they call me. If I am feeling any pain, it is already gone when they are with me.

After that, when they go and have their own things to do, I have my moments of being lonely. That is when I close my eyes in my room and I say, *"Jesus, where are you? I need you."*

I feel his warmness. A warmness comes over me and I just want to thank Jesus. I know He has got me wrapped up. I close my eyes and know God is real. And then the world is covered by God. That's how I live my life.

How Does Relying on God Bring Hope?

Sharon's favourite scripture:

"I can do all things through Christ who strengthens me."
(Phil 4:13)

Questions to consider:

1. Is there a situation in your life where you can choose to worry less and rely on God more in your current situation?

2. Are you waiting on a healing or thankful for a healing in your life?

Chapter 5

Ruth

How Hope Has Given Me a Future

Growing up in South Africa was challenging. I came to the realisation, as an adult, that I had basically been gaslit my whole life. I grew up in the environment of white supremacy which shaped a lot of my thinking as I grew up. My family were members of the Dutch Reformed Church – even though we never attended. The church was very racist during the apartheid era and I think that was an obstacle.

Seeing different skin colour was a challenge to me. That was something that God had to really change in me when I became a Christian. I've always had sympathy and empathy with people of colour. But that's different to not seeing colour. And I think a lot of people don't realise that, while they might have empathy and say they love everyone, many people judge others based on colour or race. Recognising the value in diverse cultures is a different way of thinking. That was a challenge or an obstacle in my Christian walk that I had to overcome.

I was 25 when I when I fully surrendered my life to God. And that's when God started to work in me and changed my point of view. We had been out of apartheid for about six years. This is when many people of different colours and cultures came into my life. I had a very colourful wedding. My sister was my maid of honour and I had an Indian girl and a black girl as my bridesmaids and it was sincere. I love them. They are my friends. I look at my wedding photos and acknowledge where God has taken me.

I grew up seeing the hypocrisy that was in the church and I grew up experiencing a lot of trauma in an abusive home, in every way. I remember, as a teenager going through things and thinking to myself, *"One day I want to help people like me."*

God had already put it in my heart back then to help others. I never had a problem knowing that God is real. I always said God is real.

I'm thankful that my parents made me go to church when I had to be confirmed. You had to go through 'confirmation' if you wanted to get married in church and during the last two years of schooling, my parents just dropped us off on Sundays in order to fulfil this requirement. I was very thankful for that because even though I wasn't genuine, and I saw the hypocrisy, the teaching still did something in me. It was the beginning of hearing the Word of God. I never read my Bible back then.

How Hope Has Given Me a Future

I heard the Word of God and even though the pastor was being racist, I see now that the Word of God never returns void. It doesn't matter the circumstances it's being preached in. If you are truly seeking God, you will find Him, no matter who's speaking those words.

Those are some challenges I faced because it really formed my character and I had quite a victim mentality. I struggled with empathy because of what I experienced in my family. Growing up in a household where my dad was abusive, but weak, obviously, because he's abusive. It shows a weak character. I was the one who would stand up against certain things. I became very argumentative, and I just had this thing rising up in me. I couldn't handle male authority. I had a real problem with that.

My struggle with a victim mentality continued when I had my boys. I thought that when my eldest son was born, and I finally had a diagnosis, it was because of my past sins. I had prayed for them in the womb. Both my children were born with Leber's Congenital Amaurosis (LCA) which causes them to be legally blind from birth.

> *"There are various genes that causes LCA, and due to inheriting two copies of the IQCB1 gene mutation, estimating to affect 1 in 1 million people worldwide."**

It also resulted in them further being diagnosed with Senior Loken Syndrome. This diagnosis means that the person develops kidney disease and requiring a kidney transplant usually in the first two decades of their life. My two boys are the only ones in both my husband and my extended family to have this condition as it is so rare, and yet it happened. Their condition is degenerative and my

---

* https://rarediseases.org/rare-diseases/senior-loken-syndrome/

eldest only has light perception now. My youngest son's vision is imploding which has basically left him with only tunnel vision in one eye and it is still degenerating.

I thought my children's diagnosis was a punishment from God because of past sins and even though I was sincerely repentant, I thought that God was judging me. I now see that as the lies of the devil.

I've never been angry at God. I can't even imagine being angry with God. I've just always relied on God. I think growing up in an abusive home, I would think God was there. I still pray for my parents.

I'm the second child but I was always the one trying to protect my sisters. I've just always been the protector. My younger sister is three years younger than me, and my brother is 12 years younger. My older sister was 18 when she had twins, and they grew up with us. My parents took them in, and she left them with our parents when they were 18 months old.

I found my peace in Jesus. He is peace and he is healing. I had people being very encouraging to me. I've had people praying and believing for healing for my two boys and I believe God can heal. But I do believe that he chooses not to heal sometimes. We all die from something. Some people want you to press in and believe for healing. And I think living in that and not finding your peace can really mess with your head.

I think people can start to have an issue with God and get angry at God because you believe for that healing, and people are rallying around you. And I am thankful that God gave me that peace early on. God made my children, he knit them together in the womb.

How Hope Has Given Me a Future

They are exactly as He wanted them to be, and they are my gift. They have changed me so much.

I am sometimes struck by how different my life is to what I imagined. Both my children are white cane users. One day, my husband was changing the ball on the tip of one of their canes. As he was watching a *YouTube* video on how to do it, I said to him, *"Did you ever imagine in your wildest dreams that one day you would be watching a YouTube video on how to change the ball-tip of your son's white cane?"*

We both had a good laugh about it because the roads God takes you down are always sobering and life-changing when you choose to surrender your situation to Him.

I wouldn't want my life any other way. The peace I have in Jesus is awesome.

My boys are 16 and 14 years old now. I've come to accept that God has given them to me exactly as they are for his chosen purpose. I am a parent to care for these children with special needs.

I have found my hope in Jesus. The worry I have to fight against is what is going to happen to my boys if I'm not here anymore. I'm their main carer. Even if I go out to the shops by myself, my eldest son will be worried, even when my husband reassures him that Mummy's going to come home. She is always going to come home. And I imagine that day, when one day Mummy's not going to come home and that's when my hope is knowing that we are all going to be together in eternity. That is my hope. That is the hope I hold on to.

I really do have the joy of Jesus. I prayed for it. I pray the fruit of the Spirit every day, and for 1 Cor 13:4-7

> *"Love is patient, love is kind, It does not envy, it does not boast, it is not proud. It does not dishonour others, it is not self-seeking, it is not easily angered, it keeps no record of wrongs. Love does not delight in evil but rejoices with the truth. It always protects, always trusts, always hopes, always perseveres."* (1 Corinthians 13:4-7)

My favourite part in that scripture is love "perseveres". It doesn't give up. To me, biblical love in a nutshell is love perseveres. You just don't give up. And you can only have that love when you know Jesus. I realised that I didn't know what love was until I knew Jesus. And then when I had my children, I had such a revelation of the love of God for me. And I think I always pray, *"Jesus, I want to understand what you did for me."*

If you pray for patience, God will put you in situations where you need a lot of patience. My grandmother was a praying woman. I was 13 and she gave me a Bible, and I found Isaiah, 43:1

> *"Do not fear, for I have redeemed you;*
> *I have summoned you by name; you are mine."*

That has always been a scripture I hold on to.

> *"Be anxious for nothing but in all things with prayer supplication, submit your request to God with Thanksgiving and the peace of God that surpasses all understanding will guard your hearts and minds through Christ Jesus. Whatever is true, noble right, and pure, loving, admirable, excellent praiseworthy, meditate on such things."* (Philippians 4:6-9)

I know and I love quoting that to people and the peace of God will be with you because that's the answer for anxiety, *"Be anxious for nothing,*" and then the next verse gives you the answer to anxiety. I think people miss that.

I grew up with a lot of shame. Abuse in South Africa is so accepted. I grew up with it. The statistics were hidden. I came to Australia when I was 31 years old. In South Africa, I couldn't walk down the street without sexual intimidation. It's just the norm. It's the way it was. I came here and I couldn't believe it – the difference, the freedom from abuse here.

My desire is to be a woman the way God intended me to be, and this desire was always there.

A pastor in my church told me about my husband, and asked if I would like to correspond with him. He was in Darwin and I was in South Africa. I just said *"yes"*, maybe because he was my old pastor. And I really trusted him. My husband sent me an email on the 5th of September. And the following year, the 3rd of September, we got married.

He came to meet me in person after six months. He came with a ring and he proposed. I think there were over 1,000 emails that we exchanged. And we spoke on the phone only something ridiculous like six times. The time difference made phone calls very hard to manage. The time we spent writing to each other was very beneficial in getting to know each other without the usual distractions of a courtship.

We came back to Australia after we were married in 2006. I just knew I was going to end up in Australia and I am once again in awe of how God puts His desires in your heart when you pray for His will to be done in your life.

One day in church, I saw my husband chatting with a young woman with downs syndrome. And he was so natural and just chatting to her, and she just loved the attention. The thought came to my mind, *"I wonder what it would be like to have a disabled child."*

Never did I think that it would happen to me! I had always thought, *"I couldn't do that."*

But looking at my husband, and how natural he acted towards this disabled girl, I thought, *"I think together, we could handle it."*

I now know God prepared us. I feel in hindsight that God had prepared me. God has prepared me for everything.

My hope is in Jesus. Through the grace of God, I came to realise that even though I cannot change my past, I have a choice in my future. That is the hope that was given to me when I accepted Jesus as my Lord and Saviour. I pray daily for the grace to face trials and tribulations with fortitude and forbearance and that it will leave me sweeter, better, nobler, stronger and with more humility.

To me, being more Christlike requires picking up my cross and walking the path of pain and suffering as Jesus did. Jesus came and showed us how to live, and the New Testament is literally a manual on how to deal with life's challenges through God's perspective. I know my Saviour has already overcome and I follow in His footsteps with the assurance that I never walk this path alone.

At the end of the day, to be with Him for eternity is what I live for.

Ruth's favourite scriptures:

"Be anxious for nothing but in all things with prayer supplication, submit your requests to God with Thanksgiving and the peace of God that surpasses all understanding will guard your hearts and your minds in Christ Jesus. Whatever is true, noble right, and pure, loving, admirable, excellent praiseworthy, meditate on such things." (Philippians 4:6-9)

"Love is patient, love is kind. It does not envy, it does not boast, it is not proud. It does not dishonour others, it is not self-seeking, it is not easily angered, it keeps no record of wrongs. Love does not delight in evil but rejoices with the truth. It always protects, always trusts, always hopes, always perseveres." (Corinthians 13:4-7)

"Do not fear, for I have redeemed you; I have summoned you by your name. You are mine." (Isaiah, 43:1)

Questions to consider:

1. What steps can you take to be at peace with your current challenges?

2. Is there a situation where you have to persevere?

Chapter 6

Dr Rhonda Emonson

How Does Hope Overcome Obstacles?

I grew up in a Christian home and every uncle was a minister. I gave my heart to the Lord in my early teens; played the organ most Sundays for a small congregation and participated in youth groups.

On the long weekend in June 1989, I went for a bike ride with my family. I was 16 weeks pregnant with my second child and had my three-year-old daughter in the child seat on the back of my bike.

Less than a block from home, I decided to cross the pedestrian crossing and had a strong sense to enable my daughter to remain on my bike, but for me not to ride the bike with the child seat at the rear of the bike. I exchanged bikes and went ahead solo across the pedestrian crossing and others were to follow close behind.

On the pedestrian crossing, I was hit with an incredible force by a car with faulty brakes. My head hit the windscreen and I was flown up over the car landing some distance away on the hard bitumen. The impact was so great that I obtained 13 fractures in my skull and one fracture on my forehead pierced my brain and many soft tissue injuries. Some time later, I could not understand why I was only seeing half of everybody's face and in fact, it was half of everything. In addition to the fractures and other injuries, I received what is called a Homonymous Haemopina – that is when an impact is so great on part of the brain that here is a visual deficit in half of each eye.

I do not remember being hit, although I remember a few moments before and only have 'photo memories' for a long time afterwards. I remember the physical pain and the decision not to heed medical advice to abort my unborn child at 19 weeks gestation. I remember the obstetrician saying, *"Rhonda, you will not be able to look after yourself and you will not be able to look after a newborn – my recommendation is to arrange a termination now on medical grounds."*

I respected all other medical advice, but I did not agree to them terminating my second child.

I didn't do much else other than survive at the time as I didn't have the mental clarity to know what day it was. I was in existence mode. I kept going… I kept going despite the pain and the limitations and the unwanted adjustments… I kept going because I had a three-year-old to care for and an unborn child. I had to fight, I wanted to live, I didn't want to die. I kept going because I was grateful that our lives were not taken and that God had far greater things planned. Some days it made sense and other days I wondered what it was all for, but I guess that is a normal human response.

Then in 2001 came another significant event. I was having these weird symptoms where I would have projectile vomiting and lose sensation on the side of my face, and we weren't quite sure what was happening. We went to Melbourne to visit some friends for the weekend. We'd had dinner and I stood up to go to bed and had all these symptoms, but more severely. They called an ambulance, and I went to the hospital and that's when everything started to unravel.

I was there for two weeks for extensive assessment and testing with MRI's and assessments of every description. The neurologist came up with a diagnosis of multiple sclerosis. He based his diagnosis on pathology, radiology and clinical signs.

The motions were set in place for a medical downward spiral of paralysis. I came home to start that journey with professionals talking 'doom and gloom' and asking me about what style of wheelchair I would like.

I endured the most awful injections every day for 10 years to help reverse the disease – injections that made me barely able to function. I lost my job, we had to sell our house because of the stairs and move to somewhere where there were no stairs, and my children were robbed of having their mother during their adolescence as I was often hospitalised and reacting to the immunosuppressants.

There were a lot of adjustments, but perhaps I think one of the hardest things were the reactions that I had every day to the immunosuppressants. My children had a mum who was not being able to do things at school. I was a mum who everyone talked about, *"Oh, your mum's got multiple sclerosis."*

All through this time I had the best of neurologists. The best Melbourne, Victoria could offer.

10 years had passed, and I had to see a local doctor, but he was away, so they booked me with a new doctor. I didn't want a new doctor. I needed somebody who knew my history. Anyway, I saw this doctor who said, *"I don't think you've got MS."*

I remember thinking, *"A new doctor, what would they know?"*

They sent me back to Melbourne for more tests. It was confirmed: No, I didn't have MS. Wow! It was a miracle – I was healed, without a doubt.

Medical professionals suggested that having MS and then not having MS was a medical mistake – it was a misdiagnosis even though I had 10 years of treatment from various, well-regarded neurologists.

I have copies of the MRI's. I claim it IS an absolute miracle, complete healing, not a medical mistake. During those 10 years, I'd go to altar calls for prayer. I don't know exactly when I was healed… But I know I have been healed of multiple sclerosis.

Many of the experiences I have had do not make sense to me – being hit by a car while on a bike and spending many years trying to regroup and having 10 years of treatment for multiple sclerosis. I do not understand why I have had these experiences. Some days, I do not know what to do with these experiences but I do know that I have hope for the future!

How Does Hope Overcome Obstacles?

I realise that what has happened does spur me along. The drive, the gratitude, the honour of being given life and being given the opportunity to do more and share more and to encourage others more.

God has further work for me to do. Some of that work is to encourage others, to show understanding but not to have a mightier-than-thou approach or to shout from the rooftops that my miracle was so profound that the earth moved, so to speak. The healing is ongoing and having hope that I can make progress, that I can make a difference is all part of the healing process and the job is not yet done.

I believe that my testimony can be an encouragement to others. Who would believe that someone who has had near death experiences, who has less than 50% vision, who has spent so much time in the medical system, who is not allowed to drive, who has lost their chosen career, who has experienced severe financial strain, who has missed large chunks of being a mum, could complete a PhD (recently) and stand up and speak to several hundred people at a conference?

If I hadn't had those experiences, if I hadn't experienced the miracles, would I be able to encourage you to keep going despite what life may be throwing at you?

I've relied on God's word, such as:

> *"I can do all this through him who gives me strength."*
> (Phil 4:13)

I wrote that verse out on a big piece of paper and put it under my chair. Literally! I have had scriptures on my phone as reminders, as encouragement for the days I feel emotionally wobbly.

On a day-to-day basis, a lot of my work is on self-care and relaxation strategies for those who are at risk of emotional exhaustion – especially those who professionally care for others. I am shifting my focus now to develop programs online to reach more people than I can in one-to-one sessions in my private practice. If I do the online programs well, I will have more opportunities to support more people. I'm in the right place at the right time in history to be able to do that.

Just this year, I'm finding that it is time to tell my story. I recently did a trip to the Philippines and for the first time, I got up on a public stage and shared some of my story and it had such an impact because it gave me connection with the audience. People had similar stories, but different stories. My story is no greater or less than anybody else's, but we can connect to others when we share our authentic self. I think it is time to tell the good bits and the bad bits. To share my story, to encourage others and to encourage you at this time.

The reality is that life can be tough. Even as a Christian, we can lose a marriage, lose our home, lose our career, feel discouraged or feel that there are many aspects about life that just do not feel fair or just or our fault or serve a known reason. It's not all bells and whistles. Does it mean because we have challenges, we have a lesser measure of faith? I personally don't think so. I believe that we need to have hope and we need to keep moving forward – even if it takes little steps at first.

My thinking has changed over the years about lots of things. I am thankful and grateful. Thankful that I have been given an opportunity to continue with a life that is fulfilling and of consequence. I am seizing opportunities to live a life that is honourable.

How Does Hope Overcome Obstacles?

I am grateful that I kept going, grateful that I am contributing. Grateful that the accident and the 10 years of living with multiple sclerosis are just a part of my journey, but not what defines me. However, they are part of what makes me authentic and as the physical, emotional and spiritual healing is ongoing, I am reminded of the miracles.

I am reminded of the grace of God, and I am reminded that the injuries are not 100% gone. There is enough to remind me that yes, I am a survivor, yes, I have a mission and yes, there is more work to be done. I really do think that if there was absolutely no evidence of my injuries, it would be hard to be authentic, to share and to encourage others.

I have this strong inner hope and drive and with that comes a lot of responsibility. God has given me this opportunity. Like a second chance at life, my life was not taken away.

My hope for the future now is that one day I will make sense of all of this. That I can encourage others, not to boast, but rather to be an inspiration to others, to let them know that they can move forward from what seems impossible, to have sustained faith and focus. I hope that some aspects of my journey will help you in yours.

Rhonda's favourite scriptures:

"I can do all this through him who gives me strength."
(Phil 4:13)

"Do not be anxious about anything, but in every situation, by prayer and petition, with thanksgiving, present your requests to God. ^{7} And the peace of God, which transcends all understanding, will guard your hearts and your minds in Christ Jesus." (Phil 4:6-7)

Questions to consider:

1. If you have an unexpected injury or diagnosis, what will give you hope to go on?

2. Having courage to share your testimony is a step of faith in being vulnerable. Are you able to share your story?

Chapter Seven

Amanda Nickson

How to Have Eternal Hope and Overcome the Impossible

I need hope like I need air. When I first thought about hope, I'd been let down by some people. My parents separated when I was 17 due to domestic violence. I had learned to keep quiet and to keep the peace. At that time, there seemed to be a lot of shame about being in a 'broken family'. Single parent families were not common. I learned from my Mum to be courageous, to make a move, to start again, no matter the cost, and to have hope for a better future. I was looking for hope and to the One who could give me that hope.

What are the benefits of having hope? It helps us look to the future and not dwell in the past. We're able to believe that anything is possible. There's a verse in the Bible that I often think of and meditate on – it is Isaiah 14: 31:

> *"But those who hope in the Lord will renew their strength. They will soar on wings like eagles. They will run and not grow weary, they will walk and not be faint."*

Gaining strength and being able to soar helps me to know I can have a strong and confident expectation of the future.

Some of the challenges I've had in my life have included dyslexia, my parents splitting up and later in life, suffering from anxiety and depression. I've also overcome a broken neck. But before I tell you about those stories, I want to talk about who gave me hope for the future.

Finding that I could have a personal relationship with God as a teenager made a huge difference to my future. I had a peace and purpose beyond my understanding. And there seemed to be infinite possibilities into the future. This influenced my choices in life in such things as my career, my husband, what we've done as a family and choosing to serve in churches. Several scriptures encouraged me and gave me hope. These include:

> *"For in this hope we have been saved. Christ is our source of hope."* (Romans 8:24)

> *"May the God of hope fill you with all joy and peace as you trust in Him so that you may overflow with hope, by the power of the Holy Spirit."* (Romans 15:13)

How to Have Eternal Hope and Overcome the Impossible

"Be strong and take heart all you who hope in the Lord."
(Psalm 31:24)

"I eagerly expect and hope that I will, in no way be ashamed, but will have sufficient courage, so that now as always, Christ will be exalted in my body, whether by life or by death, for to me to live is Christ and to die is gain." (Philippians 1:20)

I've thought about hope a lot and what it is. A dictionary tells me it is the aspiration or desire, expectation, aim, plan and a feeling of trust. It is a feeling of expectation and desire for a particular thing to happen. As a verb, 'hope' means we want something to happen, or to be the case, we anticipate, wait for and be hopeful of an event.

It's not where you start in life that defines you, it's where you decide to place your future. In God's hands, you are not alone.

I have been inspired by a Christian singer and songwriter known as 'Nightbirde', Jane Marczewski (1990-2022), who sang an original song on *America's Got Talent* in 2021 called *'It's OK'*. She spoke about her current journey with having cancer, which at the time of her audition was in her spine, lungs and liver. She stated that:

"I'm so much more than the bad things that happen to me...You can't wait until life isn't hard anymore before you decide to be happy."*

I fully agree with her statements. What have been my challenging experiences and obstacles that made me wonder if hope was possible?

When I first started school in grade one, it became evident very early on that I struggled. I struggled to put letters together to read

---

* https://www.youtube.com/watch?v=CZJvBfoHDko

words and to spell. My spelling was very bad. I would get two out of 20 words correct, even though I had studied the spelling list the night before. That's 18 out of 20 wrong. I was fortunate that I had a mother that picked up on this and believed that I was smart. Something wasn't working right. And she took me to be assessed and to get extra support around ways to learn to read, write and spell. I had dyslexia, a "specific learning difficulty" as it was described then.

Early into my schooling, she changed the school I was attending from a state school to a private Christian school where it was thought I would get better attention and help. My parents would do extra work with me every night of the week trying to get me to be able to read, write and spell.

For years, I hated reading. I would read the minimum I had to. By high school, I could read and write, but my spelling was always very poor. I think now, how funny it is that I love books, reading and that I am writing my fourth book. I am amazed at the place I am in now, by God's grace – fancy being an author!

Even to make it to university to do my Bachelor of Social Work degree after school seemed incredible when I think back. At the end of doing this, I was never going to study again (or so I thought) as it seemed such a struggle.

Years later, I returned to university to do post graduate study with a Master of Social Work. Then again, a few years later, I enrolled to do some research in a PhD. Who would have thought I could ever do that?

What got me through that difficult time as a child struggling with dyslexia was the belief in me and the love my parents had for me – in particular my mother, and that made a huge difference. She gave me hope that I would be able to read and spell if I persevered and didn't give up.

Many years later, I found myself doing tertiary education again; postgraduate study to do a PhD in social work. I was struggling, but this time, it was with anxiety and depression – debilitating anxiety. I needed medication and was having a hard time. I didn't believe I would ever be able to finish my studies.

I struggled with believing in myself. I thought that I wasn't good enough. I wasn't enough. I wasn't capable. I felt that I was an imposter trying to be an academic. The love and concern of close friends and family carried me over that finish line. They believed in me, and they supported me, many praying with me and for me. The scripture:

> *"I can do all things through Christ who strengthens me."*
> (Philippians 4:13)

became my mantra. I thought it was impossible for me to finish this giant task but with God, nothing is impossible.

It took me 10 years to finish, studying part time as well as working full time, with all the responsibilities for my three children and my husband working night shifts for most of those years.

A couple of years after finishing my PhD, a close friend asked me to join her book club where people read books for fun. Previously, that had been a totally foreign concept to me! I saw reading books as a chore – a task or necessity, due to studying and having to read certain academic literature. Now, I find I can read fiction and escape to foreign lands and times – a whole new world has opened to me.

I really enjoy reading. In fact, books are now one of my favourite things. I love to learn from the journeys of others. I am encouraged by stories of people of faith. This is a far cry from the young girl struggling with dyslexia for years and even as an adult, the woman who read only what she had to.

I found that I could relate to this verse in Rom 15:13:

"May the God of hope fill you with all joy and peace as you trust in Him, so that you may overflow with hope by the power of the Holy Spirit."

When I trusted God with my future, with outcomes, then I found peace and joy and an unbelievable hope for the future, despite the circumstances. It is my prayer that others will experience this hope that only God can give us and be overflowing in hope, so that it spreads and touches others.

Another situation I've had in life was in 2010 when bush walking on Hinchinbrook Island, I unexpectedly broke my neck at C6 and C7 after a fall. I didn't realise it was broken. My neck was numb and sore and my arm went limp. And I had pins and needles in my right hand. I thought I'd done something to my arm. But because I didn't seem to have a broken leg or anything that serious, I kept going.

I kept walking for another four days with an unstable neck fracture. It was a 32km hike. There were times when I felt I couldn't carry on and asked myself, *"What's wrong with me?"* I was holding my chin up with my hand because it hurt to look down. The back of my neck hurt.

I'd got to a point where I was miles behind everyone else in my group. I'd stumbled on some rocks in a creek bed and fell, landing on my bottom. I was sitting on the rocks and I said to myself, *"I can't do this."*

I just sat there for a while and thought, *"What does that really mean if I can't keep going?"*

It would mean that somebody is going to have to walk back and find me, then they are going to have to walk ahead and signal for someone to find a signal to phone for help. I would probably have to be carried out on a stretcher, then take me by a helicopter somewhere. This would be too dramatic. And then I remembered that scripture, Philippians 4:13:

"I can do all things through Christ who strengthens me."

And I just spoke those words out loud over my circumstance and took one step. I can do all things through Christ. I took another step. *"I can,"* another step, and I continued walking that walk until reaching the campsite that night. It would be another two days until we left the island, then overnight in Cardwell before a minibus trip back to Townsville.

Once we were back in Townsville, I saw my doctor and was referred for an X-ray. I had a phone call from my GP who urgently asked, *"Amanda, where are you?"*

"I'm outside the X-ray place," I replied.

"You need to go straight to Emergency. Don't look down, don't look sideways. You have an unstable neck fracture you need to go there, and they will stabilise it for you."

I remember thinking, *"That can't be right. I've been walking and stumbling and falling over for days."*

I had been literally tumbling and stumbling all the way on this walk on Hinchinbrook Island. I found out that I had a broken neck and I needed spinal surgery, and I was put in a halo brace. The disc between C6 and C7 was squashed and removed, and a spacer was put in with two bolts and a titanium plate.

Every doctor, the neurosurgeon, the nurses at the hospital all said, *"You're so lucky,"* and I'd reply, *"I don't believe in luck. I believe God protected me."*

There is no other possible explanation. I should be paraplegic, quadriplegic or dead. It's a miracle that I am here. I was only in rehabilitation a couple of days before I went home and back to work part time. A walking miracle.

I know God is the one who protected me and that's what believing in His Word, and speaking His word out loud over my circumstances did. This gave me first-hand experience of how having faith in God and trusting Him to be there for us shows that He is real. That gives me hope for the future. It doesn't matter what circumstances come my way, God is with me and cares for me.

What happens if your situation seems hopeless? What if what I am hoping for doesn't happen? God has never let me down. I know God is reliable. His timing may not always be the same as mine. But God is reliable. What if I'm in a hopeless situation? There may be seasons where we lose hope. But it's only a season and it won't be forever.

I find if I surround myself with other people of faith, they can build my faith. If I'm struggling myself, I reach out for encouragement

How to Have Eternal Hope and Overcome the Impossible

from God's Word, the Bible, and encouragement from other believers. And I talk to God about whatever my struggles are. He is with us and being in constant prayer with God is a great help.

Amanda's favourite scriptures:

"May the God of hope fill you with all joy and peace as you trust in Him, so that you may overflow with hope by the power of the Holy Spirit." (Rom 15:13)

"But those who hope in the Lord will renew their strength. They will soar on wings like eagles. They will run and not grow weary; they will walk and not be faint." (Isaiah 14:31)

"I can do all things through Christ who strengthens me." (Phil 4:13)

Questions to consider:

1. What can you now hope for and believe for?

2. Can you believe for the impossible to become possible in a particular situation or circumstance?

Chapter 8

Uma Rani Turimella

How to move from Despair to Hope

I was born and raised in South India, in the bustling city of Hyderabad. Growing up, I was blessed to have two loving sisters, Usha Rani, Joya Rani and a caring brother, Vijaya Kumar, with me being the youngest member of the family.

My father, Rama Krishnaiah Turimella, served as an administrative officer in the railways and was also known for his role as a dedicated union leader. My mother, Yesu Mani Turimella, is a teacher in a private school. Their hard work and dedication to their professions served as a constant source of inspiration to me.

Hope for The Future

My father's life was a testament to service and sacrifice, rooted in the traditional principles of communism. Coming from a family of agriculturists, he broke free from rural life and pursued job in the city in the Railways. Yet, he never forgot his roots and remained deeply connected to his village community.

Throughout his life, my father embodied the values of compassion and generosity. He understood the transformative power of education and dedicated himself to ensuring that others had access to it. Whether through financial support or free tutoring, he enabled countless individuals in his village to pursue their dreams and aspirations. As a union leader, my father was a fearless advocate for justice and equality. He fought tirelessly for the rights of workers and their families, championing causes that uplifted the marginalized and oppressed.

Above all, my father's life was a shining example of selflessness and service to others. He lived by the principle that true fulfillment comes from lifting others up and making a positive impact on the lives of those around us. His legacy continues to inspire me and countless others to strive for a better world, guided by the values of compassion, empathy and solidarity.

My mother is the epitome of selflessness and generosity, a shining example of humility and nobility. Throughout my life, she has been a pillar of strength, supporting my father and our family in every way. Her kindness knows no bounds, and her joy comes from serving others.

Our home was always open to relatives and visitors and my mother welcomed them with open arms and a warm heart. She tirelessly served them, ensuring their comfort and well-being, often going beyond to meet their needs. At times, she even sacrificed her own possessions, selling her jewellery to provide for their travel expenses.

Even today, my mother continues to cook extra food, sharing meals with anyone in need. Her acts of kindness are not just a reflection of her compassionate nature, but also a testament to her unwavering love and dedication to helping others.

My Relationship with My Siblings

The bond I share with my siblings is one of profound love and support, cultivated over years of shared experiences and devotion. Being the youngest in the family, I was showered with affection and care, with my brother and sisters often generously giving me money and gifts.

My sister, who is a surgeon, went beyond to provide for me, ensuring I had beautiful dresses and essentials. However, it was my older sister, Usha Rani who held a special place in my heart. From supporting my education to shouldering the responsibility of our family at a youthful age due to our father's health issues, she made countless sacrifices for our well-being.

Despite being miles apart, my sisters and I share a deep connection. I make sure to speak to my family every day especially spending hours with my older sister each day engaged in heartfelt conversations about everything from Bible sermons to gardening. Her unwavering presence in my life was a source of comfort and strength and I always knew I could turn to her for guidance and support.

My Education

My family always held high hopes for my future and envisioned me following in the footsteps of my accomplished siblings. With my older sister excelling as a bank manager, my brother making strides in the railways as a tradie, and my other sister a doctor, the expectation for success was palpable.

Yet, it was a conversation with my father's friend that truly ignited my passion and determination. He shared his own tale of unfulfilled dreams, highlighting the sacrifices he made to support his family, instead of pursuing higher education. His words resonated deeply within me, serving as a catalyst for my decision to pursue engineering.

Fuelled by the aspirations of my family and the encouragement of my father's friend, I studied engineering. I immersed myself in the study of electronics and communication engineering, determined to turn their dreams into reality.

My Spiritual Journey

Growing up, my family held diverse beliefs; while my mother embraced Christianity, my father leaned towards communism, and we rarely attended church services. However, we did celebrate Christmas, a cherished tradition in our home.

In seventh grade, a pivotal moment occurred when I visited a friend's house after they had just concluded a prayer meeting. Uncle Benjamin posed a question that left me feeling embarrassed – I could not articulate the meaning of Jesus Christ. He took the time to introduce Jesus Christ to me; this ignited a spark within me, prompting me to delve deeper into matters of faith.

How to move from Despair to Hope

By ninth grade, my journey with the church commenced. Bethel Church, founded by Bakht Singh, also known as Hebron Church, was close to our new home. I attended the Sunday school. I loved it so much. Since then, I never stopped going to church. Attending Sunday school became a highlight of my week and I found immense joy in learning about Christian teachings, principles and community.

It was on January 1st, 1985, during my 10th-grade year, that I personally accepted Lord Jesus Christ as my Saviour, acknowledged my sins and sought forgiveness from God. I was baptised on May 13th, 1993, under the guidance of Uncle Babu Rao, my spiritual Father, who named me Beulah, signifying the joyous relationship between God and His people.

> *"And when the Chief Shepherd appears, you will receive the crown of glory that will never fade away was the promise given to me on my baptism day."* (1 Peter 5:4)

Fear of Death

In India, Hindu funeral cremation ceremonies are deeply rooted in tradition, involving the ritualistic burning of the body, overseen by a Hindu priest and attended by male family members. Before proceeding to the burial ground, the dead body is carried by four individuals accompanied by a band. As a young child going to school alone, the sound of this procession invoked fear within me, causing me to hide until the sounds dissipated before venturing to school.

During my adolescence, when our family was constructing a new house, the burial ground served as a shortcut to our home. Despite my previous fears, my newfound faith in God alleviated my apprehensions about death. With unwavering trust in the presence of my God, I no longer hesitated to pass by even during the cremation ceremonies. At that time – although I lacked knowledge of specific Bible verses – my faith provided me with the courage and assurance needed to confront my fears head-on.

My Marriage

Despite our close friendship, Chakravarthi's proposal for marriage came as a surprise after five years of companionship. While a good man whom I deeply respected and cared for, I hesitated to accept his proposal for two significant reasons.

Firstly, our familial relationship gave me pause, causing me to question whether marrying within the family would be the right decision. Secondly, the words of 2 Corinthians 6:14-16:

> *"Do not be unequally yoked."*

weighed heavily on my heart, reminding me of the importance of being equally yoked with my partner in faith.

With these considerations in mind, I initially declined Chakravarthi's proposal, recognising the complexities of our relationship and the spiritual guidance urging caution. Despite this, Chakravarthi remained patient and understanding, respecting my decision while also expressing his unwavering commitment and love.

For another five years, our relationship evolved culminating in marriage. However, this decision was not without its challenges, as it sparked significant disagreement within our families. We found ourselves expelled from our family home, a painful experience that left me feeling as though I had betrayed my beloved sister, Usha Rani, who had always treated me like her own daughter. It was undoubtedly one of the saddest days of my life, marked by tears and heartache.

In the initial stages of my marriage, I have experienced periods of isolation, humiliation, loneliness and sadness. However, my marriage itself was a blessing. It was filled with love and support which helped me get through this emotionally challenging time, along with my continued worship and devotion to God. Steadily, I went from enduring to embracing this next chapter of my life.

> *"Weeping may stay for the night, but rejoicing comes in the morning."* (Psalm 30:5)

Workplace Challenges

Amid relentless efforts to secure a promotion, I have encountered a series of job application rejections, each one feeling like a setback. However, during this challenging period, I have found solace and inspiration in the story of Joseph, who faced rejection despite doing what was right. This narrative has taught me the importance of patience and maintaining a cheerful outlook while waiting for God's timing.

At work, my colleagues affectionately refer to me as the "work mum," a title I hold dear. It speaks to my nurturing nature and willingness to support and guide others in their professional endeavours. I have learned the value of contentment, whether in times of abundance or scarcity. It is a lesson that has grounded me and helped me appreciate the blessings in every circumstance. Philippians 4:11-12 says:

> *"I am not saying this because I am in need, for I have learned to be content whatever the circumstances. I know what it is to be*

in need, and I know what it is to have plenty. I have learned the secret of being content in any and every situation, whether well fed or hungry, whether living in plenty or in want."

There are many challenges in the life I have encountered but God was with me all the time. So many miracles happened. All glory to God!

Life in Covid: God Comforts His children

During the second wave of the COVID-19 pandemic, both my mother and my older sister, Usha Rani, contracted the virus. While my mother recovered, my sister's condition worsened rapidly, and she was taken from us and promoted to glory on May 13, 2021, just three days after falling ill. Her passing shook our family and friends to the core, as she had always been a pillar of strength in our household.

In the aftermath, grief enveloped us all. For three months, the shock and sorrow were so profound that I found it difficult to speak to my mother and brother. Instead, I relied on video calls facilitated by my nephew, Raj Kumar, to check in on them. During this time of mourning, I found solace in conversations with my doctor sister and Raj Kumar, as we sought to comfort one another with the belief that our beloved Usha Rani was now in heaven, embraced by God's eternal peace.

During that time when God took someone dear to me suddenly, controlling my emotions and communicating with my family became incredibly challenging. I deeply missed my sister, who was my greatest source of love and inspiration. Her silent encouragement to dream big continues to resonate with me.

How to move from Despair to Hope

The weight of the pain was overwhelming. To cope, I immersed myself in work during the day, but the nights were the hardest. Tears would flow incessantly, and it felt like an insurmountable burden. In those moments, I found solace in the messages and worship songs of Dr. Asher Andrew. Through his teachings and music, God comforted me, reminding me of the scripture from Psalms 34:1:

"I will bless the Lord at all times;
His praise shall continually be in my mouth."

All praise and worship belong to God, even during sorrow and loss.

The impact of COVID-19 has been immeasurable, with the loss of numerous family members, including my beloved aunt, who passed away on May 22, 2021, following the loss of my sister. During this trying time, gestures of sympathy and support, such as receiving flowers from iSee Church and my workplace, served as comforting reminders of love during the grief.

Amidst the challenges, staying connected with family through Zoom meetings became a lifeline, providing solace during moments of profound sorrow and the daunting task of launching a new business. The delays and uncertainties surrounding the business venture added to the mounting stress and anxiety, leading my husband to resign from his job and seek temporary employment. However, the generosity of friends who contributed to our start-up costs and the unwavering support of our church community and family provided much-needed comfort and encouragement.

In the depths of despair, I turned to prayer and scripture, finding solace and strength in the promises of God. Each day presented new trials and uncertainties, accompanied by sleepless nights filled with tears and fervent prayers for divine intervention. Yet, amidst the turmoil, there were moments of transformation and renewal. Witnessing my husband embrace Jesus Christ as his personal Saviour on August 11, 2021, marked a profound turning point in our journey of faith.

With the support of our close friends, we celebrated a soft launch of our restaurant after three months of lease negotiations. However, the journey remained tumultuous, leaving us physically and emotionally exhausted. Amidst the highs and lows, God granted me boldness and peace, guiding us through the storm with unwavering grace and mercy. When God is preparing for the impossibilities to change to possibilities, your brokenness prepares you. My promise in 2022: *"The fruit of your womb is blessed and the crops of your land and the young of your livestock- the calves of your herds and the lambs of your flocks."* (Deut 28:4)

The Lord blessed me with my kids – Brian as a school captain and Cherrie did very well in her university studies.

Through the grace of God, I embarked on a journey to reunite with my family for my sister's first death anniversary. During a stopover in Dubai, I found unexpected solace with my nephew Raj Kumar's family. Spending precious moments with his children, Joy and Sam, deepened our bond and together, we embarked on the next leg of the journey, arriving in India on May 13, 2022.

Upon my return, I faced numerous challenges in the construction of my sister's grave. Yet, amidst the trials, I felt the reassuring presence of God, guiding me through every obstacle. With unwavering faith, I persevered, knowing that His grace would sustain me.

Moved by the love and support of my family, I made a heartfelt decision to visit India every year, ensuring I am present to comfort my mother and honour my sister's memory on her death anniversary. This commitment is a testament to the enduring bonds of family and the profound impact of love and remembrance. In every step, I am reminded of God's steadfast presence and His unending grace, guiding me through life's trials and blessings.

Little Jasmine Joy Whom I Loved Ascended to Glory

The Lord already knew that I would go through the situation and gave me this promise in 2023 in Phil 4:13:

> *"Rejoice in the Lord always and*
> *again I say rejoice in the Lord."*

During the days where I was organising my trip back home to commemorate the second death anniversary of my sister, I heard that my great-niece was diagnosed with Leukemia.

As I prepared to board my flight for the memorial, devastating news reached me: My heart broke at the realisation of our loss. Her sudden and subsequent passing within a month left our family shattered. On May 9, 2023, little Joy ascended to glory, leaving behind a void that could never be filled.

Yet, amidst the grief, the outpouring of prayers and support from friends and family was comforting. Within minutes, loved ones responded with blood donations during her treatment, a testament to the love and compassion that surrounded us during our darkest hour.

During little Joy's battle, Raj Kumar and Annie (my nephew and niece) demonstrated unwavering faith and devotion as parents through constant prayers and fasting during her time in the hospital. Though I initially felt unable to attend the funeral, I found the strength, by God's grace, to be present at the memorial service. In that moment, I clung to the assurance that little Joy had completed her journey and was now in the arms of the Lord.

Despite the profound grief that surrounded us, I sought solace in the fact that my brokenness led me to surrender to it all to the Lord Jesus Christ. Through this, I found peace and purpose, understanding that nothing in this world truly matters except our relationship with God. The sudden loss of little Joy served as a stark reminder of the fragility of life and the importance of cherishing every moment.

At my son Brian's year 12 graduation, his poignant speech resonated deeply with me, as he urged kindness toward others, regardless of personal feelings. Inspired by his words, I intend to keep his quote close, reminding myself to embody kindness in all aspects of life.

> *"Please be kind. Be kind to the one you like and be kind to the one you do not."* (Brain Gali)

As I reflect on this in the year 2024, I am committed to incorporating Brian's wisdom into my vision board, serving as a daily reminder of the power of compassion and empathy.

Always Be Grateful

I am deeply thankful for the grace of God, who has shown me love and forgiveness aside from my shortcomings and mistakes. Despite my flaws and moments of weakness, God's unwavering love remains constant, and I find solace in knowing that I can always turn to Him. I am blessed to have a supportive family, both within my church community and across borders, as well as friends who have stood by me through thick and thin.

The values instilled in me by my family – such as the importance of the Word of God, prayer, faith, forgiveness, kindness, respect, education, and hard work –have shaped my character and influenced every aspect of my life. Their unwavering support and example have moulded me into the person I am today: a mother, sister, friend, wife, and more.

The simple act of someone taking the time to listen or reaching out to resolve an issue demonstrates true value and care. Just as the Bible teaches us that Jesus came not to be served, but to serve, we are reminded of the importance of prioritising the needs of others above our own. It's essential to always remember and appreciate those who have extended a helping hand along our journey.

Learning to Live by Faith

When life gets hard, when we don't have any strength, we can always find a ray of hope.

> *"Then David and the people who were with him raised their voices and wept until they had no more strength. David was greatly distressed, lost everything the city is burnt, their wives and son's and daughter taken captive."* (1 Samuel 30: 4-6)

> *"But David found strength in the LORD his God."*
> (I Sam 30:6)

> *"Therefore do not throw away your confidence, which has a great reward. I always tried to find my strength from my God."* (Hebrews 10:35)

Hope for The Future

I got the answer for the question: Why should we live?

According to Psalms 118:17, our purpose for living is to recount the deeds of the Lord. The verse declares:

> *"I shall not die, but I shall live and recount the deeds of the Lord."*

Thus, our existence is meant to be a testimony to God's mighty works and faithfulness.

I am resolute in my commitment to love God for as long as I live and to share His love with others, motivating and encouraging them, particularly in addressing social issues and making a positive impact on people's lives. My faith in God is the foundation of my strength, guiding me each day as I listen to His voice and praise Him. One verse that resonates deeply with me is Romans 12:12 which teaches me to:

> *"Be joyful in hope, patient in affliction, and faithful in prayer."*

The Christian journey is often a battle against the forces of evil, both within us and in the world around us. In anticipation of our eventual departure from this world, we find solace in the promise of a forever home with the One we trust. In that eternal realm, we will be joyfully reunited with our loved ones who embraced the salvation offered by our Lord Jesus Christ. Together with our vast church family, we will dwell in the safety of heaven. My aspiration echoes the sentiment of Matthew 25:21 (NKJV):

> *"His Lord said to him, 'Well done, good and faithful servant; you were faithful over a few things, I will make you ruler over many things. Enter into the joy of your lord."*

May we always remember that we are God's cherished priority. Each of us is deeply loved, and through Christ, we are set free from the bondage of sin.

My Desire and My Prayer

One thing that holds a special place in my heart is helping children whose parents struggle with addiction. Education is the key to breaking the cycle of hardship, and I am enthusiastic about providing opportunities for these children to thrive. Education has been my own redeeming quality, opening doors and shaping my future in ways I could never have imagined.

As I gaze into the future, my deepest longing is to lead a life that glorifies God, reflecting His boundless love and grace. My ultimate aspiration is to be reunited with my Lord and Saviour Jesus Christ when my earthly journey concludes.

2 Timothy 4:7-8 is a passage that resonates deeply within me. It inspires me to strive towards a future where, like the apostle Paul, I can confidently declare:

I have fought the good fight, I have finished the race, I have kept the faith.

These words encapsulate the essence of a life dedicated to serving God faithfully, persevering through trials, and remaining steadfast in belief. My aspiration is to echo Paul's sentiment, knowing that by God's grace, I have fulfilled my purpose and remained unwavering in my devotion.

How did I overcome and have hope in my despair?

Good Company

I surrounded myself with uplifting individuals who share the same faith and gained strength and support.

Practice What You Believe

Since I became a Christian, even though I was not perfect, my life was not right with God at times, I never stopped going to church.

Hear Only God's Voice

I have overcome my despair by persistently obeying God's voice by listening to a video by a preacher. I have never compromised God's commandments.

I used to sing songs to God all the time, irrespective of the situation. I have overcome by praying loudly that I can do all things through Christ who strengthens me, and with the assurance that no weapon formed shall prosper.

Expect Only from God

God has taught me to expect nothing from anyone, for expectations unmet breed disappointment. For what others offer becomes a cherished bonus, a sprinkle of grace upon life's journey. Yet, if the offering falls short, there is no bitterness, no disappointment. And in the embrace of divine provision, there is peace – a peace that surpasses understanding, a peace that reigns even in the face of unmet expectations.

Ownership and Responsibility

I learnt the simple principle that this is my responsibility and I take the ownership. Whatever God entrusted and given to me in this world – it could be my job or raising my kids – I try to do it whole-heartedly, with joy.

Avoiding Self-Pity

I try to avoid self-pity. If we allow self-pity in life, it opens doors for depression and ultimately it leads you to lose hope. Satan will try to get you to lose hope. Instead, I started focusing on the promises of God.

The Power of Service and Kindness

In the solitude of challenges faced in the initial days of my visit to Australia, the written words of love from a husband across distant lands became lifelines.

Clarify your vision for the future

This year, I attended a workshop for women. It was the first time in my life that I did a vision board that helped me to realise who am I, the real me, what I need and what I want to become. Then I started my baby steps to achieve my goals, made a to-do list and learnt to celebrate my achievements.

Forgiveness

I have learnt forgiveness which has become a pathway to healing and liberation.

Uma's favourite scripture:

"The joy of the Lord is my strength." (Nehemiah 8:10)

Questions to consider:

1. Can you start singing and praising despite the circumstances you are in? Put on some songs of praise and worship.

2. Are there some people you need to forgive in your life? Forgive them.

Chapter 9

Jill Sutcliffe Everett

How We Can Have Hope Because God Has a Plan

A key scripture that I have always hung onto since I became a Christian is Jeremiah 29:11:

> *"For I know the plans I have for you declares the Lord, plans to give you a hope and a future."*

Not getting married wasn't necessarily a conscious decision of mine, but I was never ever going to marry the first person that came along. My upbringing was very ordinary, stable, secure and loving. My mum and dad's life revolved around work, work and more work. I was raised to be determined, believing that I was capable and competent to do anything that I put my mind to.

I think my family had this picture that I would go to university, get my teaching degree, meet somebody, get married and have children. I didn't want to settle for those expectations on me – I wanted to get out and see the world!

Initially, I did the teaching degree, as from when I was little, I'd always only ever wanted to be a teacher. I'd been teaching for about six weeks as a Year Three teacher and there was an infant mistress who turned me off teaching right from the start. It was sad.

I thought to myself, *"What have I done?"*

It was the time when the education department had an oversupply of teachers. They were offering teachers to take almost as much leave as you liked. Once you had done two years teaching, you could take leave. I decided I was going to take six months leave and go traveling in Europe, which I did.

Once back, I thought there's so much more to the world than Europe – I'll travel some more. I taught the minimum amount required, 12 months, before I could have more leave. Then I took two years leave.

It was during the two years overseas that I had my first encounter with God in Africa. Growing up I had gone to Sunday school, but in Africa, I met this group of people for whom Jesus was real. They were talking about Jesus and how Jesus did this for me and Jesus did that. That wasn't what I knew about Jesus in the stories I had heard. I made my first real steps towards Christianity there. I prayed, Jesus, whatever it is that those people have got, that's what I want.

How We Can Have Hope Because God Has a Plan

When I came home again, I was transferred to Lucinda. I was in a place where I knew nobody. I had to make friends, so I got involved in the church there. But I still knew I didn't want to teach for the rest of my life.

But that's when this verse, Jer 29:11:

> *"For I know the plans I have for you, declares the Lord…*
> *Plans to give you a hope and a future."*

became a promise for me. Even as a young Christian, I trusted that God had a plan and that was going to be better than what I've got, because I had no idea what else I wanted to do. While in Lucinda, I was involved in the Uniting Church and in their Bible studies. I was going to church, but it was mostly a social outlet for me because it was either you went to church or you went to the pub on Sunday night, so I went to church.

I was transferred back to the Burdekin (Ayr) and got involved in the Home Hill Uniting Church that I grew up in and I was in the young adults group. During a camp one Easter long weekend, the leader said to us, *"What does Jesus mean to you? Get yourself in pairs and go off and have a discussion with each other about what Jesus means to you."*

I remember thinking, *"That's a personal question! You don't ask people questions like that!"*

However, it really made me think, what does Jesus mean to me?

The church had a programme called the 'Emmaus Walk'. I did that and when I came back, I got baptized. And then, I still didn't know what I wanted to do for the rest of my life. Because I knew that teaching wasn't what I wanted to do. So, I changed from teaching and did a stint in Life Education, but this wasn't really what I wanted to do either.

I'd moved to Townsville when I got a job with Life Education and I knew that God was talking to me about going to Bible College. I was sharing a place with another woman, but I wanted my own place. I just really felt as if God was saying, buy a house and love it. It was not my intention. I was going to get a little van in the caravan park. That's where I was going to live for the rest of my life. I asked God to show me in a way, talk to me in a way that I will know that this is the right house for me.

He took me out to the property at Rasmussen and I'm walking through it and there were Bibles all over the place in the house. I called it the Rainbow House because when I first saw it, all the rooms were different colours. Then while at Bible Study, there was some talk about the sign that God gave to Noah of the Covenant which was the rainbow. I said to myself, *"Okay, I'm buying the Rainbow House."*

The next day I went in and offered lower than what they were asking for and they accepted it. Suddenly I thought, *"God, I'm going to Bible College in six months' time. What am I doing buying a house and putting myself into debt when I am going to Bible College?"*

Well, probably six to eight weeks later, my parents rang me up and said, *"We've got something for you."*

A relative had given my parents $10,000 for each of their children – for me and both my brothers. And so, that just covered all my expenses for the next two years while I was going to Bible college. All the repayments! It was so completely out of the blue, I knew it was God's blessing as I had walked the path he had for me.

How We Can Have Hope Because God Has a Plan

I went to Calvary Bible College and at that time, God was doing a lot of work on me – rubbing off the rough edges and all that sort of thing. It was a Diploma of Bible and Christian Ministry.

The first trip to Iran happened during that time. I still didn't really know what I was going to do. One day at the church it was announced that a Pastor was going on a trip to Iran and who wanted to come? I responded, *"Yes!"*

It took about six to 12 months to organize this trip and there was a group of eight of us who went. I loved it, doing missions fitted in with my love for travel. That first trip to Iran was in the late 1990s. It was a good 10 years later that I went over to Iran and then, Turkey for four years.

I'd have been about 32 years old with that first trip. We called it a prayer trip. We weren't there to evangelize or get anybody arrested or anything like that. We visited a church in Tehran, an Armenian Church. There are different people groups in Iran and the Armenian community who are allowed to practice a Christian religion, but the Persian people aren't allowed to convert to Christianity. I guess God put Iran on my heart – I had a real passion for the people there.

At the end of Bible college, I did some supply teaching just to keep the money coming in. One day when I was driving home, I had no excitement. I hadn't been in a regular classroom for four years. It felt like I had been teaching for about 10 years. I thought, like a sign from God, that going back to teaching would be just going back. It wasn't the future for me. So, I was looking for work. This was over the Christmas holidays, and I saw an ad in the paper for prison officers.

I thought to myself, *"God, something's got to work out here."*

I don't think I was even on the dole at that point. I was paying off the house. On a Saturday, when jobs were in the paper, I was looking for work. And I said, *"God, you've got to speak to me here, what am I going to do? I need a job."* I was going to a new church the next day, close to where I lived, the Christian Outreach Centre. I said, *"Speak to me through this church."*

I was the new person that everybody was coming up to and saying hello to and I met this lady, Kay. I told her that I was looking for work and she said, *"You should come and work where I work."*

I said, *"What do you do?"*

"I'm a prison officer at the jail. I've worked there for five years."

So, I applied and much to my disbelief, I got the job. However, I wanted to be able to support people more than what the work as a prison officer offered. The jail was very much about punishment. That is when I started looking at social work.

I was at the Christian Outreach Centre for 15 years, and the mission's director there. I was very involved with promoting missions and the church did some short-term mission trips to Cambodia during that time. Whilst I was there, God was putting it on my heart again to go to Iran again. The church said we'll pray for you, and another young woman from the church, Emily, and I went to Iran. We went as visitors and felt that God put us there to be with just one family.

We spent a couple of days in Tehran. Then we caught the train at about five o'clock in the afternoon. Then about an hour and a half later, the train was coming to a stop. And there's this guy walking through the train saying what sounded like, *"No mas no mas,"* and everybody's getting off the train and Emily and I are looking at each other. We had no idea what he meant. Anyway, we got off and some people were going towards a golden mosque. It was time to pray (for the Muslims there), so the train had stopped for everybody to get off the train to pray.

We just laughed when we eventually worked it out because we had no idea what was going on. Then, we went to Mashhad, the most holy city for Muslims in Iran. Everybody wore the full hijab and were on pilgrimage to visit the big mosque that was a holy place to go to and pray. We went shopping and wore head coverings.

We met this guy at our hotel who was a taxi driver. We asked him to take us for a tour around and we got to know him quite well, because he was taking us out each day. He took us for a day trip and brought his wife along and his youngest son. We spent the whole day with them visiting different tourist sites.

That night, they invited us back to their place to have dinner and we got to speak to them about what we believed and why we believed. They spoke English, enough to have those simple conversations. We felt that this trip was just for this family, that for whatever reason, that was our purpose for being there. And we came home again, and our church continued to pray for this family. I have no idea what happened to them and never heard from them again.

Sometime later, I heard about YWAM (Youth with a Mission) having an outreach for Muslims on the Gold Coast. There are a lot of Muslims from the Middle East who go to the Gold Coast each year for their summer, our winter over here, on holidays. YWAM was training people for reaching out to Muslims. I went to that. We were to build relationship with them, have a coffee, and share our faith. After connecting with the trainers who put me in touch with some other people and because I had been to Iran, I had a job in Iran. The process took 12 to 18 months.

The job was to work with a non-government organization. I was going to be running a community centre for Afghan refugees that had been living in Iran for two or three generations. All the people who worked in the organisation had to be Iranians. We happened to employ Christian Iranians. My assistant, who spoke English quite well, was also running a house church, so I got involved with that with him.

He rang me up one day and said, *"Jill, I'm just letting you know I'm going home to clean the house. I'll explain it later. I'll only be about an hour or so."*

He was going home to move all the Bibles out of his house. He had to get rid of them. When he got to work later, he explained that many of his colleagues had all been arrested overnight and were in jail. It was because they were all involved in house churches. He kept saying, *"I've got to get rid of these Bibles out of my house."*

I said, *"Well, what are you going to do with them?"*

"I'm going to take them to your place," he replied.

Billy Graham often said that if Christianity was illegal, would they have enough evidence to arrest you? And I remember thinking, *"Yes, there is!"*

So slowly but surely over the next couple of days, all those Bibles ended up at my house. I had a bed that had this section where you could lift it up like a lid and it had this big space underneath. It was hidden and not obvious. It didn't look like it had a space underneath. It just looked like part of a bed. I became this woman with copies of Farsi Bibles under my bed (in the bed), sleeping on them every night. Nobody ever found them.

Being there was a good experience. I regularly attended a German church for expats on a Friday as Friday is the holiday there. I did some guest speaking with an Iranian house church and youth group. It was exciting to be a part of their groups.

One day, we were doing an activity, teaching about hearing God's voice, and one of these young people, said, *"Why are we playing these stupid games anyway?"*

I said, *"You're living in a country where you could be walking down the street and if you tell the wrong person that you're a Christian, you could end up in jail."*

You were rarely a nominal Christian over there. You were either fully committed to your beliefs or you were not because the risk of being a Christian over there was just too big. I don't think some of these young kids realised it because they'd grown up in homes where their parents were Christians and they talked about being Christians. It was relatively normal for them at home, but it wasn't the norm within the community.

I was there for two years and a lot of the church people that I had contact with either ended up in jail, or they escaped to Turkey. I worked with a man and his wife who decided to go to Turkey as asylum seekers. They'd been there for about six months and then I went there. They had to go to the UN in Ankara to seek asylum and then they got sent to a regional city.

I joined them in Turkey. He was working for an organisation and was able to start a church. I was teaching English, and we planted an

Iranian church with consisted mainly of Iranian Christians escaping persecution in Iran. We had a Bible study for some Afghans who had converted, but even in Turkey, the Afghans did not feel safe to be open about their Christian faith because of the persecution they would face amongst the Afghan community and fear of reprisal for their families still in Afghanistan and Iran.

I did that for about 18 months, then due to various circumstances, I felt that it was time to come home.

This was when I was in my 40s. When I came back to Townsville from Turkey and Iran, I got the job as the co-ordinator of a women's homelessness shelter. I did that for three years. During that time, I went to Connect Church and then iSEE church and I started doing a social work course. The work at the women's shelter was mostly rewarding and at times, very challenging. But I knew that God had a plan, and the plan was for hope and to give me a future.

I have travelled to 60+ countries as a tourist. To me, it was a natural extension to this, once I became a Christian, that I would want to do overseas missionary type work.

Looking back, my wanting to travel was a bit of a rebellious thing. I wanted to get out and see the world and have fun and do things that other people don't do. At that time, I had never met anyone from the Burdekin who had done any significant overseas travel. I wanted to see the world, but the Burdekin has always been home, and I've always come back.

Reflecting on my life now, I can see that God's had a plan in all the travel and various jobs that I have had, and still has... For my whole life. I'm glad I did what I did before I was married, because I don't think I'd have done any of that travel if I had married young. And I wouldn't be doing it now.

In my 20s, I explored the world. In my 30s, I bought a house and went to Bible college. In my 40s, I embarked on missions in Iran and Turkey and in my 50s, I got married.

I have been able to do all this travel and missions work as a single female, with no limits, because I just believed I was doing what God was leading and directing me to do. I think you've got to keep moving in your Christian walk and not get stuck. If you keep walking, God can direct you and if you walk on the wrong track God can point you back on the right track.

I look at the steps that took place when I ultimately ended up going and living in Iran for two years – the way God worked that out. If I hadn't taken the step and gone to the Gold Coast for the training, and if I hadn't spoken to the trainer and said I've been to Iran, would he still have introduced me to these people who were over there?

I can see where the house came in again as I can see God's plan right back to buying my house. If I hadn't bought the house, I wouldn't have had the equity that gave me the funds to fund myself to live in Iran and Turkey.

God helped plan right back then because when I was buying the house, it always had it in the back of my mind that I needed the repayments to be low enough that if I ever wanted to rent it out, the rent would cover the repayments.

In thinking about what are my plans for the future and my hope now, I can see God working in both my husband Scot's and my life. I don't know where God's leading us exactly, but I know that because we both love God and trust God, that in the end, despite whatever obstacles we may face, that God will prosper us and will give us hope. Then we will be a blessing for other people.

For me, marrying a non-Christian was never a consideration. Soon after we got married, Scot and I joined the Salvation Army church, which has opened doors for us to serve God, that may not have opened elsewhere.

It is similar to when you first become a Christian and you realise that God is working in your life and you've got that level of excitement; I can see that in Scot and myself, right now.

Whether we'll end up ministering together or whether we'll always have our own separate things, I know that God is in control. He's got a plan. And as we're faithful to whatever He's calling us to right now, that will continue to open doors in the future. That's my hope now – to be faithful with what I have, what you believe God has called you to. If you're off track a bit, God will get you back on track again.

Jill's favourite scriptures:

"For I know the plans I have for you declares the Lord, plans to give you a hope and a future." (Jeremiah 29:11)

"And we know that in all things God works for the good of those who love him, who have been called according to his purpose." (Romans 8:28)

"For I have learned to be content whatever the circumstances." (Phil 4:11)

Questions to Consider:

1. What plans and purposes do you believe God has for you?

2. Have you ever felt limited by the expectations of others on what you should or shouldn't be doing with your life? What can you do about this?

Chapter 10

Jenni Sedon

How to Move from Hopelessness to Hope for the Future

"I cry out, 'My splendour is gone! Everything I had hoped for from the Lord is lost!' The thought of my suffering and homelessness is bitter beyond words. I will never forget this awful time, as I grieve over my loss. Yet I still dare to hope when I remember this: The faithful love of the Lord never ends! His mercies never cease."
(Lamentations 3:18-22 (NLT)

Christmas Day 2006 was the biggest, most traumatic challenge – and change – I have ever had to experience in my entire life. The suddenness of it was incomprehensible and this was the day that shattered all my dreams and my whole world changed.

The hopelessness and despair I felt left me numb and lost in all my emotions that I had never ever experienced before. My body shut down. I experienced a loss of taste; loss of appetite and I lost 10 kilos. I was already very small and my weight fell down to 48kg.

The main challenge for me was the flashbacks and I couldn't stop reliving the powerfulness of the flashbacks of what had happened. It was too raw. I kept seeing what I had seen over and over again. Going to bed at night and sleeping was really hard, that initially was a big challenge for me. I was only able to sleep two or three hours a night. This turned my world into a place of tiredness and exhaustion, trying to work, trying to move forward but I couldn't escape the tiredness that consumed me.

Late in the evening of Christmas Day 2006, I was watching a movie at my daughter's house when we received a phone call to say that my house was on fire. We raced around there as it was only a five-minute drive from my daughter's house. I saw smoke billowing and when I arrived, there were huge flames engulfing the house.

I looked and I could hear my daughter who was there with me asking, *"Has anyone seen my father?"* and that's when I realised that my husband wasn't there.

At the side of the house, we had a granny flat adjacent to the house where Rick would watch TV, so I presumed he was asleep in the TV room. I instantly grabbed a friend and a guy that was standing nearby, and we ran to that side of the property and pushed down a fence. As that fence came tumbling down so too did my world as I knew it. Nothing could have prepared me for the shock of the confronting scene.

How to Move from Hopelessness to Hope for the Future

I came to find that Rick was dead and that he had taken his own life. When I saw my husband was dead, I just dropped to my knees.

This is the scene: My house is on fire and my husband is dead.

It was very confronting. Then the reality of it hit me... Rick starting the fire was just unthinkable, yet that was what appeared to have happened and then he took his own life.

I realised that one of my daughters was there and then I had to tell her that her dad wasn't with us anymore and I told her what he had done. I couldn't let my daughter witness what I had witnessed. I went into protective mode.

Telling my daughter was certainly the hardest thing to do in my role as a mother.

I had lost my husband of 28 years and had lost my home at the same time. It was very traumatic. The hopelessness I felt. The shock triggered tides of endless emotions pulling me out to sea, emotions I had never ever experienced before. I realise that suicide is very complicated as you have questions – all these unanswered questions which would keep me awake at night.

It was easy in a situation like this to have pity parties. I wanted to find answers to unanswerable questions. There was an intense pain watching my daughters and knowing there was no way that I could protect them from the grief they were going through or give them answers. My daughters were aged 19 and 21 years old at the time.

What helped me was that I did have very supportive and loving friends and family. I have a very strong bond with my girls – even though my heart was aching for them having to go through this

– that was something that we went through together. I do believe that God had us in survival mode.

Another thing that helped me was the time I spend alone with God reading His word, the Bible. I have had a faith in Jesus since I was about seven years old.

I received a Christmas card about a week before Christmas with the most unusual verse on it and I had thought that my friend had lost the plot when I got it. I'd also had the same verse in my quiet time alone with God. This verse is not a verse you would write on a Christmas card. It was:

> *"When you go through deep waters, I will be with you. When you go through rivers of difficulty, you will not drown. When you walk through the fire of oppression, you will not be burnt up, the flames will not consume you."* (Isaiah 43:2, NLT)

How incredible. I had that in my own quiet-time, and I got it on a Christmas card, not that I remembered straight away. It was about a week after the fire, and I remembered this verse that had been sent to me. It was God bringing it to my attention. So that gave me hope. It made me realise too, that God knew the events that were going to take place. The chapter goes on to talk about redeeming – I have redeemed you.

It made me realise, well, I believe that God saved my life. There's a lot more to that part of the story. It made me realise that God knew what was going to happen. And for me that verse gave me encouragement.

Reflecting on life now, I know that God's got great things in store for me. I appreciate every day because you don't know when your day is going to change. I am enjoying the love of family and friends. Just seize the moment. I think back to what I've been through, and I realised how important it is to talk to yourself and to tell yourself to enjoy the moments.

My hope for the future is to be encouraging to others who go through a hard time.

> *"I cry out, 'My splendour is gone! Everything I hoped for from the Lord is lost!' The thought of my suffering and homelessness is bitter beyond words. I will never forget this awful time, as I grieve over my loss. Yet I still dare to hope when I remember this: The faithful love of the Lord never ends, his mercies never cease."* (Lamentations 3:18 – 22, NLT)

I just can't believe that God speaks to me through his word. That it's okay to cry and feel sorry for yourself, but I think it's one of the things that I have learned. Because if that's what you are feeling, God is okay with that.

 I just knew that God was with me, the verse in Isaiah 43:2 meant I knew I was loved by God. I didn't know how I was going to get through it, but I knew somehow I would get through it.

When I was in that time of grief, it was like time stood still. I hated anybody saying, *"Time is a great healer"* because it made me think, *"Oh my goodness, if only they knew what they were saying,"* as being in it, I couldn't see anything past what I was going through. I was just flooded with emotions.

Reflecting on my faith since then, I guess it changed in a way where I realised how much God talks to me through the Word. How God could use a Christmas card to talk to me – that makes me laugh. Or

God can use a movie to talk to me. I love that God's gone further than just being in a box or a church on Sunday.

Looking back, Rick suffered with mental health, but at the time when you're married, I just thought he's getting older, and couldn't cope as well. In hindsight, there were some signs like he didn't like the phone ringing and other little weird things. I guess you don't really notice things happening because he was the most unlikely person that you thought would do it (suicide).

One of the answers that did come was from a neighbour who had moved our rubbish bin and saw in it a totally empty bottle of scotch. Somebody had given Rick a bottle of scotch as a thank you for something he'd done, and it looked as if he had drunk it all. Whether he had drank that while I'd been out, we don't really know because he wasn't working at the time. Rick and alcohol were never a good combination.

Due to the circumstances of how the fire had started, there was cause for concern that I may not have received an insurance claim. I had to trust God. The sleepless nights did bring about a dream that I had seen a stamp of approval and finally, the insurance ended up getting paid out. There was the worry about whether or not the insurance company was going to pay me or not. I learned that you have to just trust God.

> *"You keep track of all my sorrows. You have collected all my tears in your bottle. You have recorded each one in your book."*
> (Psalm 56:8)

This verse made me realise that every tear is worth shedding when they're precious to God like that. Can you believe that? It's special to God!! Every tear is not wasted. I used to joke with God that there was a Lake Jenni in heaven.

How to Move from Hopelessness to Hope for the Future

For me, it feels more personal when God talks to me through the Bible. He is keeping track of everything. Every tear. Wow. Then God must have my name with a huge bottle of tears.

This gave me more empathy when I worked in the hospital and pastoral care. Life experience can make us more relatable to people. Not that you could ever take the pain away, but I think it's been a bittersweet lesson. I wouldn't want other people to go through it. God at this time was my anchor when I was feeling so many emotions.

For the future, I'm waiting on God. I'm happy to have an adventure with God and to know that he brings you through and I would like to think that the best is yet to come.

Jenni's favourite scriptures:

"When you pass through the waters, I will be with you; and when you pass through the rivers, they will not sweep over you. When you walk through the fire, you will not be burned; the flames will not set you ablaze." (Isaiah 43:2)

"I cry out, 'My splendour is gone! Everything I had hoped for from the Lord is lost!' The thought of my suffering and homelessness is bitter beyond words. I will never forget this awful time, as I grieve over my loss. Yet I still dare to hope when I remember this: The faithful love of the Lord never ends! His mercies never cease." (Lamentations 3:18-22)

"You number my wanderings; put my tears into Your bottle; are they not in Your book?" (Psalm 56:8, NKJV)

Questions to consider:

1. What are ways you could support someone who experiences sudden and unexpected grief and loss?

2. Remembering that grief affects everyone differently and there is no set time frame for recovery, how might you be kind to yourself in considering any loss you have experienced?

Chapter 11

Soleil Nyirabyiza

How to Be Confident for the Future

I was born in Rwanda and came to Australia as a refugee with my family in 2011 when I was nine years old. This was with my parents and four brothers and sisters. Mum had three more children in Australia – so I am the third eldest child of eight children.

I know there was the war in Rwanda in the 1990s – the genocide of the Tutsis with the Hutus. My parents were in the Congo and had to escape back to Rwanda. Living in Rwanda, I remember living in a village and going to school. Our village was very simple, with houses made of very strong sticks and mud.

I would come home from school at lunch time, eat lunch with my family and go back to school. I think school finished late in the afternoon. As kids, we would get together in the neighbourhood and entertain ourselves with games. There is one where you draw boxes in the dirt and jump – hopscotch. There were no parks, or entertainment for kids like there is here. We only had ourselves. There was no TV or *Netflix*. We also spent a lot of time in church.

My mum was the one that used to work because my dad has been sick. My mum has been our provider ever since I can remember. My dad often gets sick with mental illness and is on medication. Before, he used to be a truck driver and he could speak French, English and Kinya Rwandan. My dad is smart.

At home in Rwanda, we spoke Kinya Rwandan. When we arrived here in Townsville, we had to learn English. We could navigate around as Dad could speak English, but for the rest of us, it was starting from zero. I had never spoken English before and knew no English at all.

I started in primary school, and I learned English as a second language while other kids in my class were learning other things. I was in a class with students the same age as me but starting way behind with English. It was intimidating. I was different to the other kids, and I didn't speak the language. I didn't have any friends and really went through a hard time.

My brother and I were the ones that started together at Vincent Primary School. I don't think I'm shy, but I thought for a long time I was shy because in school I was very quiet. It was not knowing enough of the language – you need language to communicate.

How to Be Confident for the Future

I started in Grade 4 and it wasn't until about Grade 9 that I felt comfortable with myself speaking. It took five years. Before that, I was observing and looking at my environment. It was a tough environment. Kids can be mean. Some kids are brutal. I was very scared of some kids because I would be sitting in class, and they would pick on me and bully me. I didn't know about bullying – it just felt like they didn't like me. That was that was my experience. It was tough.

I feel that I have been trying to survive from that point on until I was about 18 or 19. My whole time in Australia until then. Once I turned 18, and I was legally an adult, that's when I started being a little more okay and feeling like 'I've got this.' I felt a little bit more balanced.

Before then, there was all this pressure. I had to think about my family. You had to think about school and what am I going to do with my life. I didn't know what I was doing. Even in high school, they're telling you, what pathway do you want to go to? They want you to make all these decisions.

I was pretty lost and confused. It was only when I became an adult, that is when I could say, okay, what do I want for myself, outside of my family, outside what people expect me to do. There were all these expectations. I guess when I could think for myself, then it was: I can make decisions for what I want. It was exciting.

When we arrived in Townsville we had support, because when you come to Australia as a refugee, there is a lot of support. Australia has so many opportunities. But I felt very alone.

I've had church my whole life. Now that I'm an adult, it's a different thing. Because when you're young, you do things because you're told to do them by your parents. That's a whole different thing. I still felt alone. Even though we had the church community, even though we had people coming to teach us English and take us out whenever there were events. The feeling was good.

This ties into what gives me hope for the future now. I'm 22 now and being in church helped me to be closer to God. And that's when I began searching for myself. I started seeking God for myself. A friend, Esther, helped me get closer to God. I was questioning the way God plays a role in my life, where I am, where I've been. God has a purpose for me, and I'm not here by mistake. And just because we've been through a lot of things, not all good, things will be better. I think once I was established in God, I started to think what if I give some time. What can I bring to the world and then it gives me hope that I can do something with my life and with myself.

I feel that God sent Esther my way when I really needed her, because I honestly felt I was lost. I was so angry with my life, with my parents, because my parents had the same mindset from Africa. They hadn't adjusted to being in this country, to Australian culture. I felt we had a lot of clashes and arguments and misunderstanding because we were living in an Australian culture – although I've grown up through the Australian cultural system.

I felt that when you're young, and you're trying to figure out who you are, I was in the Australian culture with friends whose experiences were not what was acceptable to my parents. My parents thought that I was trying to copy the Australian culture and they were against that. I found it difficult because to me, I had left much of the African culture behind in Africa when we came here. For me, I felt they were trying to bring something that didn't bring value to me. We had a lot of conflict in my family around this, and it stayed with me for a long time.

How to Be Confident for the Future

I was trying to find myself, but my parents were always challenging me, *"Why are you trying to be like this?"*

The conflict impacted me emotionally and I had a lot of resentment towards my mum. Now being an adult, I realise it is what it is. It put a little wedge between me and my parents.

Finding God gave me hope. I might not be able to change them, but I can have forgiveness and see what is in the past is the past. Let's leave it there and then move forward. It took me a long time to get to this point.

Now, as an adult, there are a lot of things I can do for myself. I feel like when you're a child, you don't really have the power to speak your mind. I'm in a place where I'm finding I have a voice. If my parents say something to me, with the friends that I have or whatever, I can speak up now. When I was 13 or 14 years old, those early teenage years, it was hard because I didn't know why my parents were telling me to be a certain way. Then at school, I'd try to fit in. I'd have friends if I fitted in, so it was a mental battle with myself, trying to figure out my identity.

Now I'm building myself financially, working full time. When you are in high school, you have to choose your path of where to go. Are you going to do a trade; are you going to go to uni? What are you going to do? Are you going to go to TAFE? I felt the pressure and I didn't know what I wanted.

I went to uni and I failed my course. I thought I was a failure and that I was never going to be able to do it. That was a lot. Then what were my other options? I went back to work, which is now what I'm doing. I didn't go to uni because I wanted to; I went to uni because my friends were going to uni and I felt as if I had been left behind.

If you don't have education, then you have nothing in this world. That's how I felt.

I was doing a Diploma of Higher Education to hopefully pass and then do nursing. Don't ask me why nursing. It just seemed like the right choice. Everybody else thought so. It was not easy. I failed and felt like a loser. But I'm going to be somebody. I feel like I've been placing my identity on things or maybe on an occupation rather than who I am.

Now I feel that I'm in a better place with myself. To me, before, it was well, if they can do it, I can do it too. I didn't realise, not everything is for you and maybe your skills or maybe your talents are in something else. Finding yourself and just knowing who you are, that helps. I'm in a place where I can be honest with myself and say, *"I'm good at this."* or *"I'm not good at this."*

And it's okay that I'm not good at some things. Maybe that is not for me. As a female in an African family, my family's mindset as I was growing up, as a woman, was that I should know how to take care of a family by doing the things you need to know to keep a house clean and cooking and things like that. And I resented that because I felt – what if I don't want to do that? I was a little bit rebellious.

I was seeing that in the Australian culture, some men do those roles too. I suppose I was challenging those gender role stereotypes where certain things are expected. I ended up choosing to move out of home for a while and live independently and that did not fit well with African cultural expectations. My parents were against it.

After taking time away and finding myself I realised, I do want a family. Yes, I want a family. But I want to do it my way. I want to bring more of an authenticity to it. If I'm the type of woman who would rather have a man cook sometimes – he can. If I want to sit down and rest while he does, that is alright. I decided that I do want love and I do want a family, but I want to do it my way. I decided to move back home, which made my parents very happy.

Finding God for myself and finding faith for myself has helped me. I now know more of the Bible, and I am aware of some Christians being hypocritical. I've been disappointed that some Christian people are very judgmental. When I used to hear preaching about God before, I did not know the whole truth. Because I didn't read the Bible for myself. I thought it was just a very ancient book and who needed it anyway. When I read the Bible for myself, I found myself there. Before, I used to think the Bible is for the parents.

Knowing God now and what He says about families, knowing what he says about women, I have found the truth is good. It is helpful knowing what the Bible says. The Bible does say, in John 8:32:

> *"Then you will know the truth,*
> *and the truth will set you free."*

No one is to judge others. I suppose we're all humans that make mistakes and none of us are perfect. We just try to follow as best we can.

I found myself in the Bible. I love that. Because I feel that it's about the favour of God. When I look at my life, and how much anger and resentment I had in my heart, I'm so thankful that God could still do something in me – and give me hope.

I relate well to the story of Ruth in the Bible – she was a widow in a foreign country that nobody knew. I can relate to her because

I left the country that I knew, and I've come to a new country. I didn't even speak the language and I had to learn to make friends and figure out who I was and find a career before figuring out my life. It was stressful.

Then when you put God in the middle, I could say, *"God, I don't know what I'm doing with my life, or with myself, so please help me."*

I believe He will – God can still do something for me because He did it for Ruth. The book of Ruth is one I can use and one I meditate on.

Whenever something is not going right, or I've messed up somewhere, I always think that God can turn it around. As the verse Rom 8:28 says:

> *"And we know that in all things God works for the good of those who love him, who have been called according to his purpose."*

It is not the end of my life. I'm going to be fine. Look where I've come from.

I'm running my life now – where I go, what I do, who I talk to. I have a freedom and choices now. I never used to feel that way about my life. I don't know if this is an age thing or God. Or both. I don't know if other 22-year-olds feel the way that I do now. I feel very comfortable and good. I'm excited to see what God is going to do next.

Soleil's favourite scriptures:

"And we know that in all things God works for the good of those who love him, who have been called according to his purpose." (Rom 8:28)

"'For I know the plans I have for you,' declares the Lord, *'Plans to prosper you and not to harm you, plans to give you hope and a future.'"* (Jeremiah 29:11)

Questions to consider:

1. How can you decide your own future, despite peer pressure and the expectations of others?

2. Do you believe that God can turn your circumstances around and work them for your good?

Chapter 12

Ann-Marie McCann

How Hope Can Bring Provision

The year that I turned 15, my parents passed away. They died six months apart. My mum had breast cancer that she'd been fighting for years. She passed first. My dad passed away five months later. I was the youngest of four children and the only girl. My brothers were much older.

Dad was an alcoholic and by the time I was five, he was a complete mess in our lives. 10 years later when my mum died, my eldest brother applied to become my legal guardian. He was the Australian Vice Consul to Hawaii at the time and had been on numerous postings around the world and in consulates with Foreign Affairs. My other brothers were in Australia – one was in Sydney; one was in Canberra. My dad was in the family home, but he couldn't look after me.

My eldest brother came back to Australia for me, and I flew back to Hawaii to live with him and his family. It was in the next five months that my dad passed. He died from cirrhosis of the liver which he had been battling. That was a real shock – just the timing of it. I stayed in Hawaii for the next six months. My brother was great, but very busy with work. My sister-in-law was a socialite. I didn't feel like I really measured up as she had very high standards.

I was quite lonely in Hawaii as I had left all my friends. That was a challenge. It was a different lifestyle too, quite formal. It's not as laid back as Australia – especially the community I was part of.

I kept a diary, and I wrote things about how lonely and homesick I was. I also wrote about my feelings toward my sister-in-law which weren't great. She found it and it was decided that it would be better if I went back to Australia.

I moved back to Canberra and went to live with another brother and his family in my family home. My brother and I had a great relationship, but I had a very difficult time with my sister-in-law there, too. It was not good. She was very difficult to be very around. I felt like an outsider in what had been my family home.

I was 16 years old now, I had boyfriends and everything that went along with being that age. It was probably very difficult for her as well – especially considering that she had two little girls and her own family life. I was eating out most of the week at different places as I was really unhappy in the house. When I turned 17, rather than finish the last three months of school, I left and moved to Sydney.

How Hope Can Bring Provision

My other brother was a chartered accountant who lived in Sydney. I had been traveling back and forth to stay with him and his family since I was about eight years old. I loved it there. In school holidays, my mum would send me on the plane and I had a great relationship with them. I stayed with them for the next 18 months. It was awesome. We had a great time. They just made me feel part of the family. It was totally different.

I can see that having the three brothers and being able to live with them, although it was difficult especially in the first few years, it was such a blessing in my life. I also see it as an answer to my mother's prayers. She had known she was dying and constantly prayed for me.

When I turned 18, it was time to stand on my own two feet. I got my own place and moved out. I became independent and was training to be a beauty therapist. Not long after this, I met this guy who was searching for God. He told me that he was searching for God on our first date. He said, *"I'm gonna find God."*

And I remember thinking, *"Who says that on a first date?"*

I had a semi-religious upbringing. My mother was a sincere Catholic. She'd become a Catholic to marry my father. My dad wasn't a sincere Catholic at all, but those were the rules. He never went to church. My mother took me though.

Interestingly enough, just before my mother passed away, I remember that there were these people that used to come to the house and talk to us about the Holy Spirit and being baptized in the Holy Spirit. I think it was the charismatic Catholic movement. Mum was very interested. She used to talk to me about God a lot. Although after she passed away, I never went to church.

When I met this guy in Sydney who was searching for God, I was certainly not interested in God, but I thought it was interesting. We ended up moving in together and living together for about six months. He wanted to see Perth and so did I. By now, however, I didn't want to stay with him. He suggested that we drive there – we'll see a bit of Australia on the way but I thought, *"Okay, but when we get there, I'll just disappear, and start a new life on my own."*

On the way, we had to go via Canberra to say goodbye to my brother and his family. That's when I found out that this sister-in-law that I had found so difficult to get along with was now 'born again'. When we got there, she was a completely different person. In the past, she wanted nothing to do with my boyfriends etc and I had been telling my boyfriend, *"You will love my brother but don't worry about my sister-in-law. Just hang out with my brother. He smokes dope. You'll get on great."*

When we got there, she seemed so nice. I looked at her and wondered if this was the same person? My boyfriend was looking at me as she was so nice and wondering what I had been talking about. Then she started talking to us about God. It began to dawn on me that she was now a Christian. My boyfriend was really interested, but I was trying to get used to her being this 'new' person.

My boyfriend suddenly decided to sell the car and hitch hike to Perth. He was so impulsive! I thought it would be so dangerous over the Nullabor, but being a Canadian, he had no idea how far and dangerous that could be, and that's what he wanted to do. He left the day before me, saying he'd see me there.

I decided to catch the Greyhound bus instead. I still had another day with my sister-in-law. When I was leaving, she gave me a Bible saying that it had changed her life and she really wanted me to read it.

On the bus, I read through the whole Bible. As I read it, I recall thinking how amazing it was. I really liked it. I liked what Jesus was saying. I believed that this held the answers to life; it was so alive to me.

I think prior to reading that Bible and eventually becoming born again, I probably would have gone down a path as a human rights activist or lawyer. I had a passion for helping people, wanting to help people who were oppressed – especially women. When I started reading the Bible, I started really thinking, *"This is the answer, but it's not just a temporary answer."*

Without God, I thought I could really help people. I can stand up to unrighteousness and inequality and get laws changed, and we can make differences. But then what difference is it going to really make in the light of eternity? The more I read, the more I saw an eternal reward and an eternal outcome. That was so inspiring to me. This was a completely new outlook for me.

I trained as a beauty therapist in Sydney. I had got a little bit of money from my father passing away and I paid to do beauty therapy, and then I was going to look for a job in Perth.

I was working all this out in my mind. By the time I got there, I had read through nearly the whole Bible. I was reading it, loving it, taking it down to the beach with me and just reading and thinking, *"I love this."*

I planned to stay in a backpackers for a few weeks while I looked for a house. It was here that my ex-boyfriend showed up. He just walked in. I had just finished telling a girl I was single.

He had all these plans for us. I wanted to speak to him alone, so we went walking on Scarborough Beach. I told him that I don't want to be with him and he responded, *"I want to get married. Let's get married."*

While I'm thinking, *"No, no, no."*

As we're walking along, we turned up a road off the beach and walked one block and there's a whole team of young people standing out in front of a YMCA building which was being used as a church. All these young people were going to a concert there and so they immediately start talking to us about God. They invited us to the concert. But I didn't want to be there with this boyfriend.

We said we'd look around the building and maybe come back the next day. They introduced us to another guy who showed us around and told us about the church and that was Neil (who I later married). We went back the next day, and we both got saved.

After hearing the preaching, I realised that reading the whole Bible had prepared me. I wanted this new life.

I stayed with my boyfriend for another three months. I think that God kept us together – especially in my case to get to that point of finding salvation. Then I moved into a place with some Christian girls, and he moved in with some Christian guys.

Six months after becoming a Christian, Neil, who I had met that first day, asked me to go out with him. We were married within that next year.

All my wanting to make a difference in the world and to do something to help others, fitted in with helping people find Christ and eternal life. Neil had been a Christian for 18 months when he met me. By the time we got married, Neil felt called to preach. I felt that was a confirmation on my call to reach others too.

We moved to Sydney to plant a church and then to Glasgow, Scotland. After that, we moved to Newcastle, South Africa and finally, New Zealand. I realised it was easy for us to leave because we had no family ties where we were. We wanted to go and do whatever God had for us. It was still huge - these were big moves.

Looking back, in my early Christianity, I believed that everything that happened was a test of faith. I think that's how my mindset was. When we moved to Glasgow, that was a big step. Within two weeks of arriving, the bass guitarist at church was murdered. He was only 17 years old; he was trying to defend his mum outside a pub. He was due to get married in two weeks' time. It was unbelievable. That set the tone for the next seven years.

We took over a church. I was 23 and Neil was 24 at the time. I was also 38 weeks pregnant. We were on this big adventure. When we got there, there was supposed to be a house for us and a church building. We didn't know the rent on the house and the church building had been paid six months in advance, but when we got there, everything was overdue. The six months payment was up and, suddenly we were being evicted from the house.

We had taken a house with furniture that belonged to the house. We didn't have any furniture. We had to get out of that house and I was about to have a baby. We were trying to get support but we couldn't find a rental. Our sponsoring people did not understand the situation.

Everything was way too expensive. Neil is a UK citizen. He decided to go to the housing office and apply for a house. We realised it was going to take us years to be on the list. You had to get points, so there's five points for being in the area for 10 years. There's five points for having a certain number of kids. We were not going to get a place.

We eventually found this place, which was in a tenement, like the ones in New York. It had a central stairway with people living on each side. People there used to steal everything. They stole the piping. There was no furniture, no curtains and we had a new baby, our son Robbie.

There were drug addicts in the apartments, and in the stairwell, there was blood spattered everywhere. It was nowhere near what I had expected.

There were so many challenges. There was the fact that we were probably the only people in the street that had a car. It was getting broken into, and all this other stuff kept happening. We needed to get out of this area and get into another area. Neil was trying to find work outside of the position as basically, the church didn't have the money to support us. The people sponsoring us were not sending any money and we had believed that the church was supposed to be self-sufficient.

Neil was trying to reach people in Australia, but his contact person just avoided us. There was no other support. That was the scenario.

Over the seven years we were there, we had tried to leave about three times. In the last six months, after six years of trials and many disappointments, we had a release date. Neil was working in a service station overnight. I was working too. We had moved to a better area – it was nice. We had Holly now too, our third child. We were looking forward to moving back to Australia.

How Hope Can Bring Provision

What kept me going through all these challenging times was hearing from God by reading the scriptures or learning about other believers in God, which always raised my faith. What really has kept me going is the verses. I've always been strengthened by them. It's like seeing God move so often during these times that you have got to think to yourself that He is the only way. There is no other help coming. I was getting a strong faith muscle because I was working out (my faith) and being encouraged by seeing the results of the workout.

God provided – we had no support from the church.

Neil would get invited to preach in other churches and they would give some finance to him which helped greatly.

One particular miracle happened there which greatly helped my faith. A lady came to church and was looking for healing for a neck injury. She came to us as a last resort. We prayed for her, but she did not get healed and never came back to church.

Amazingly though and ages later, two envelopes came under the door of the church. One envelope was for the church – it was about £3,000. And the other envelope was for us personally. This was at a time that we had absolutely nothing and so many needs. We were desperate. We hadn't seen her for months and out of the blue, she provided for us. We saw God move like this in many miraculous ways.

Some of Neil's family background are Scottish gypsies. Sometimes, the gypsies would just come to the church and when they come into an area, they would bring services to the church. They doubled the church numbers when they came to town. They would come and then they would do whatever was needed.

I saw so much during those first years as a fairly new Christian and early in our marriage. So much. It was a radical testimony of God's provision.

Now after nearly 40 years that I've been travelling and pastoring churches with Neil, I have called myself a 'willing accomplice'. God has always met our family's needs and it's always been evidence of His love. We would be moving in one direction then; God opened the door to us somewhere else.

One time we had been preparing to go to China, but God moved us to South Africa. One of the most challenging things for me has been leaving somewhere. When you invest a lot of yourself in a place and then God moves you, you feel it. People are sad and you are sad, but it's the nature of the kingdom. Then I'm reminded that God is overall and he's everywhere. We have hopefully had an impact and been impacted by the people we have served. We've had a role in each other's worlds. That is what I treasure. And you can still have contact with them, even 30 years later.

In our life now, I feel that Neil and I are in a good place. We're kind of a bit free in the sense that we're not tied to anything. There was probably one time where I thought when we came back to Australia, that we were all going to be in one place. I thought it might be near Brisbane with a family home and all the kids will be there with the grandkids.

But it didn't work out that way. They've moved around and are doing different things. Our son is in New Zealand, one daughter is in Perth and our other daughter in Brisbane.

And God still has a plan for us. The journey continues.

How Hope Can Bring Provision

We plan to move to Scotland, starting with looking at Edinburgh and we will see how we feel. We have already been back to Glasgow but will not go there again. It would be too much. Everything seems a little tainted there – it was such a struggle. We have a history in Scotland and Edinburgh might just be the place. We know that God has a way of moving you in the direction he chooses, so we are open to that as well.

It could be that we do something philanthropic – we want to help people. I'm praying to go where God is leading us, in whatever direction that is.

Neil recently had open heart surgery, and one of the surgeon's said that the bypass should keep him going for another 20 years or so. It seemed that God has confirmed that He still has things for us to do. We are open. It will be exciting to see where these next steps of faith will lead us.

Ann-Marie's favourite scriptures:

"'Yes,' Jesus replied, 'and I assure you that everyone who has given up house or brothers or sisters or mother or father or children or property, for my sake and for the Good News, will receive now in return a hundred times as many houses, brothers, sisters, mothers, children, and property—along with persecution. And in the world to come that person will have eternal life.'" (Mark 10:29-30)

"Whether you turn to the right or to the left, your ears will hear a voice behind you, saying, 'This is the way; walk in it.'" (Is 30:21)

"This is what the Lord says: 'Stop at the crossroads and look around. Ask for the old, godly way, and walk in it. Travel its path, and you will find rest for your souls.'" (Jer 6:16)

Questions to consider:

1. Have you had a challenge of having to leave one situation and start again in a new place/job/circumstance. What things have helped you to settle in the new place?

2. Have you heard from God when reading the Bible? Are there particular verses that strengthen your faith and hope? Consider writing out these verses as a reminder of God's faithfulness in times of challenges.

Afterward

Congratulations on reading *Hope for the Future*. I trust that you have been inspired and encouraged. Are you ready to live with hope for your future and move forward in the plans and purposes God has for you?

I have an important question to ask you. Do you know Jesus Christ as your personal Lord and Saviour? Are you confident in your own eternal hope and eternal destination? You can be!

Are you ready now to put things right between yourself and God? Perhaps you used to believe and have a close personal relationship with God, but there has been some time away from God? The Bible teaches that:

> *"All have sinned and fall short of the glory of God."*
> (Romans 3:23)

Sin is simply our separation from God. Romans 6:23 states that:

> *"The wages of sin is death, but the gift of God is eternal life in Christ Jesus our Lord."*

Jesus has made a way for us to be able to restore our relationship with God. John 11:25-26 states:

> *"Jesus said to her, 'I am the resurrection and the life. The one who believes in me will live, even though they die; and whoever lives by believing in me will never die. Do you believe this?'"*

If you would like to have a new life and a fresh start with Jesus as your Lord and Saviour, it is as simple as having this conversation, just speaking directly with God. You can repeat these words or say something similar:

> *"Thank you, Lord Jesus, that you died for my sins. Forgive me for all I have done wrong and for not having you as the Lord of my life. I accept you now, Jesus, as my Lord and Saviour. Help me to follow you and live for you. Amen."*

Congratulations! You have restored your relationship with God. This is the most important step in our lives – it means you can be assured of eternal life with Him. You can have an eternal hope.

To build your faith and to live with expectant hope, spend time getting to know the Bible and reading, studying and learning some of the scripture will help build your spiritual foundations. Spend regular time in prayer, having conversations with God – He wants to have a close relationship with you.

Find people who can encourage you in your faith and you them. This could include finding a local church that you can be part of. Look for a church that is friendly and helps you to grow in faith with good teaching. Ask God to guide you in what your next steps are.

Afterward

More resources to help you grow in faith on your journey in life are available on my website: http://www.amandanickson.com.au/

To access Bibles online and search by keywords, visit https://www.biblegateway.com

Additional Information and Resources

For domestic and family violence support in Australia:

DVConnect Womensline: 1800 811 811
DVConnect Mensline: 1800 600 636

Support for victims of abuse (including sexual assault, child abuse) in Queensland:

https://www.qld.gov.au/community/getting-support-health-social-issue/support-victims-abuse

For recovery from childhood abuse:

Bravehearts (Queensland) offer support for adult survivors of child sexual abuse via their Information and Support Line 1800 272 831

https://bravehearts.org.au/get-help/support-adult-survivors/support-us/

For carers support:

https://www.carersaustralia.com.au/support-for-carers/carer-gateway/

For disability support:

https://www.disabilitygateway.gov.au/
https://www.ndis.gov.au/

For support with grief:

https://www.grief.org.au/ga/ga/Support/Support_Groups.aspx

Grief Australia at 0392652100 /Free call number at 1800642066. *https://griefline.org.au/*

For mental health support:

For mental health and psychological support: *www.beyondblue.org.au*

For depression: *https://www.blackdoginstitute.org.au/*

For counselling and support:

To find a social worker, Look at *https://www.aasw.asn.au/find-a-social-worker/search/*
To find a psychologist, *https://psychology.org.au/about-us/contact-us/aps-find-a-psych*
Or *https://ccaa.net.au/* to find a Christian Counsellor
Dr. Caroline Leaf has written several books including *Helping our Mental Health and Emotional Wellbeing* and *Cleaning Up Your Mental Mess*. Her website also has some other podcasts, apps and resources: *www.drleaf.com*

Discussion Questions For a Book Club or Discussion Group

1. In Chapter 1, Samantha overcame incredible odds to excel in school in foster care and later to go on to complete university to become a teacher and be able to teach in areas she loved. She decided she wanted a different future to her own past and chose to be positive and optimistic despite some setbacks. What is holding you back from hopes you have for the future you want? How can you choose to be positive about the future?

2. Struggling to find enough care and support for independent living and study, Karene was determined to attend university anyway. Do you have hopes and goals you could start on, even if everything isn't quite in place? What steps could you take?

3. Julie trusted God in everything, despite numerous challenges. She is now able to work as an artist, something that seemed impossible for a long time. Is there a hope or dream that you

Hope for the Future

have lost sight of – perhaps the timing wasn't right before, that you could step into now?

4. Despite feeling some shame and embarrassment, Sharon came back to church when she needed support and to be more reliant on God in her life. Are there circumstances in your life now that could be pointing you back to God? What can you do?

5. Ruth experienced child abuse and lived with shame until she found Jesus and was able to have a new start in life as a new creation. Are there things from your past holding you back? How can you let go of the hold of these things and move forward with new hope for the future?

6. Ruth accepts that her children, born with rare medical conditions, are exactly as God created them to be. She has a peace in the situation of caring for her children with special needs. How can you come to a place of acceptance and peace about challenges in your life?

7. In Chapter 6, Rhonda had to move house, change careers, and live in survival mode while recovering from injuries and medical treatments. She is now grateful to be alive and for the opportunities she has. What things are you grateful for in your life, despite the challenges and struggles you may be currently facing?

8. In Chapter 7, Amanda came through a time of anxiety and depression and was able to finish some study that seemed impossible to her. She believed a verse, Phil 4:13: *"I can do all things through Christ who strengthens me"* and spoke it out loud over her circumstances, hoping the situation would change. She spoke the same verse over her physical challenges when

walking with an unstable neck fracture. What situations can you believe this verse for in your life today?

9. Uma experienced unexpected grief and its devastating impact, yet she found that the joy of the Lord is her strength. How can you find joy and strength despite unexpected events?

10. Jill did not conform to limiting expectations and as a single female, took big steps of faith to live in Iran and Turkey. What steps of faith can you take? Can you think bigger and not limit the possibilities of God's plans for your life?

11. Jenni's devastating grief as a survivor of suicide (the one left behind) is hard to imagine. Yet Jenni now sees life is good and that God has treasured every tear she has shed. How does knowing God has kept every tear bring comfort for hard times you have been through?

12. Soleil experienced isolation and bullying in a new country where the culture and language were different, and it took her years to feel comfortable and that she belonged. Have you felt as if you didn't belong to a culture, or a workplace, or a region? How can you connect to others and feel safe? Is society's culture different to Christian culture? In what culture do you feel most comfortable?

13. Ann-Marie first found out about Jesus as the way, the truth and the life reading a bible. Where can we find out the truth and have eternal hope and purpose? Are you willing and able to share this hope with others?

Biographies

Ann-Marie McCann

Ann-Marie was born in the Snowy Mountains of NSW. She is a mother of three children and has seven grandchildren. What is important to Ann-Marie is to love God, love her family and to love her neighbour as herself. Her vision is to inspire others to live for Jesus, protect children and champion families.

Amanda Nickson

See the 'About the Author' section to find out more about Amanda.

Jenni Sedon

Jenni was born in New Zealand and arrived in Australia in the late 80s. She is a mother of two girls and a grandmother to four grandchildren. At present, she is a co-manager of a small resort with her eldest daughter on the tropical Magnetic Island.

Jill Sutcliffe Everett

Jill was born and grew up in the sugar cane farming communities of Ayr and Home Hill – where her grandparents and great grandparents moved to the Burdekin District over 100 years ago and Jill grew up with many cousins, aunts, uncles, and other extended family. She did well enough at school to achieve her childhood dream of becoming a schoolteacher, graduating from JCU in 1987. Over the next few decades, she went on to complete a diploma in Bible and Christian Ministries in 2001, Bachelor of Education in 2005 and a Master of Social Work in 2019. Jill married for the first time in 2022, and currently works as a social worker in community development. She looks forward to continuing walking with God, seeking his plans and purposes for her life.

Julie Mengel

Julie was born on the South Coast of NSW. In her early years, she travelled extensively working for Qantas in Sydney. Moving to Townsville, she completed a Visual Arts degree and a Grad Dip of Teaching (tertiary), where she taught art for 17 years as a single mother of two. Now married and retired, Julie lives on the Sunshine Coast where she creates art in her beautiful bush studio. Inspired by her relationship with God, Julie works with cold wax and collage. Her aim is to evoke and interpret the presence of God.

Karene Gravener

Karene was born and raised in the Burdekin. At 24, she came to Townsville to study social work. This was more than a personal decision – it was a call of God. A faith step for things that were to come. Helping people is Karene's passion and she has worked in a variety of roles across the 19 years she has been practicing social work. She has discovered that advocacy and helping others discover their story is what she is most passionate about. Karene is married and is the mother of two wonderful children and knows that her life is in God's hands and her family gives her hope that cannot be shaken.

Rhonda Emonson

Rhonda is a wife, a mother of two and a grandmother of two. Rhonda's personal journey has been impacted by two major (and unrelated) life-changing, physical, medical episodes; one in 1989 and another in 2001. Each episode required multiple hospital admissions, time away from family, rehabilitation, unplanned changes in career, learning to be resilient and taking time to 'review' life and ponder on what is really important. Along with many others, Rhonda understands that adversity can come in many unexpected forms. She believes, *"We have the option to be consumed by life-changing events or to make the decision to move forward and continue to live a life aligned with our values and purpose."*

Ruth*

Ruth is privileged to be the wife of a wonderful godly man and mother to two amazing young men aged 14 and 16 years. She was born and raised in South Africa and swept off her feet to Darwin 17 years ago when she met her husband. Growing up, she had big dreams and ambitions, but those soon faded into obscurity when she fell in love with Jesus at age 25. Knowing God and being the woman He sees her to be is now Ruth's life's goal, with her daily prayer being, *"Lord, let Your will become the desire of my heart."*

Samantha Jo Leonoski (nee Leonard)

Samantha is currently on maternity leave, living in the United Arab Emirates. She is a wife, married to Andrew, mother to Lydia (17) and Evelyn (five months), stepmother to Sophie (13), Ruby (11) and Bailey (9) and a secondary high school teacher with a school located on the Gold Coast in Queensland. She has completed a dual degree in Education and in Science at Sunshine Coast University graduating in 2015. She majored in Health and Physical Education (HPE) and minored in English. Samantha's aspiration is to encourage the best in others and allow people to see their own worth and potential – no matter their circumstances. Samantha aims to continue to grow intellectually to continue to help others into the future and to support her family.

Sharon Henderson

Sharon was born in Port Moresby, Papua New Guinea. Her family is from the gulf area where she grew up. Sharon has lived in Australia for 40 years and in Townsville since 2007. She is a mother to seven children, five girls and two boys and a grandmother to four grandchildren, one girl and three boys.

Soleil Nyirabyiza

Soleil is currently 22 years old, loves God and every day, she wakes with the passion to pursue Him. She is working full-time to support her goals while waiting on God to show her the next steps of her journey. Soleil enjoys a good book with a cup of tea and music means everything to her.

Uma Rani Turimella

Uma was born in Hyderabad, India. She migrated to Australia in 2004. She is a wife to Chakravarthi Gali and mother to two children, Cherrie and Brian. She has a Bachelor of Engineering and a Master of Information and Communication Technology, completed at Griffith University. She currently works in IT and has chosen a joyous attitude, despite the challenges life has sent her way. In each struggle in life, she faces with resilience, faith, and the unwavering belief that through God, every challenge becomes a stepping stone toward beauty and growth. She believes, *"Each day becomes a canvas, painted by the hands of God, unveiling beauty in His perfect timing. Lessons in self-worth emerge from failures, rejections, and the trials of life – learning to expect only from the Almighty, while embracing the unexpected as blessings."*

About the Author

Dr Amanda M Nickson is a wife, mother, social worker, Christian pastor, author and speaker.

Amanda was born and raised in Sydney with her parents (until their separation when she was 17) and younger sister. Amanda went to the University of New South Wales to study a Bachelor of Social Work; was actively involved in her local church youth group, beach missions and enjoyed bushwalking. She started working in social work in western Sydney before moving to Central Queensland.

Amanda chose to do social work as her profession as an extension of her Christian faith, being able to help and serve others at their point of need. She has worked in a variety of positions in government, non-government organisations, academia and private practices. She currently runs her own business in training, supervision, social work services and organizational consultancy. She has a Master of Social Work and a PhD from James Cook University.

In 2023, Amanda was ordained as a minister with the Australian Christian Churches (ACC). Her Christian faith and beliefs are at the core of everything she does, and she also has a Diploma of Leadership from Alphacrucis College. Amanda's Christian ministry includes workshops on faith, building resilience, thriving with purpose and creating your vision, as well as being a speaker at Women's Conferences and a guest speaker at churches and for other organisations.

She provides professional pastoral supervision to pastors and chaplains. Amanda also produces podcasts, does radio interviews and provides materials and courses on her website *https://www.amandanickson.com.au/* to encourage people's faith and to bring hope.

In this book, Amanda highlights a group of inspirational women whose faith in God has given them hope for the future, often despite challenges and difficulties. Her vision is to encourage others that no matter what is happening in your life, God has a plan and a future for you. There is hope.

Amanda has been a Christian for over 40 years and has served as a leader in various positions in her local church. She is a registered supervisor with Chaplaincy Australia and Scripture Union. Her passion is to encourage others in their journey of faith and to help bring people to a closer personal relationship with God.

Today, Amanda lives in Townsville with her husband, one of her three adult children, her dog Scruffy and her cat Kitty. She loves catching up with friends with a cup of tea and making time to walk in nature – especially in beautiful national parks nearby and those further afield.

Other Books by the Author

Amanda Nickson (2022) *The Resilient Leader: How to beat being overwhelmed and burnout for sustainable leadership*, Diamond Creek, Victoria; Ultimate World Publishing.

Amanda Nickson (2022) Chapter 5: *Amanda's Story – An extraordinary life* in Rhonda Emonson *Not Defined by Adversity: Stories of faith and resilience from those who help others*, Penrith NSW; Mosh Pit Publishing.

Amanda Nickson (2020) *Living by Faith: How the impossible becomes possible with God*, Diamond Creek, Victoria; Ultimate World Publishing.

Amanda M Nickson, Margaret-Anne Carter and Abraham P. Francis (2020) *Supervision and Professional Development in Social Work Practice*, New Delhi, India; Sage

Amanda Nickson (2021) Chapter 15: *Supervision in isolated and rural settings*, in O'Donoghue, K and Engelbrecht, L *The Routledge International Handbook of Social Work Supervision*, Oxon and New York, Routledge.

Acknowledgements

I am excited and heartened that this book has become a reality and I pray that it brings you great inspiration and courage to do all that God has for you.

First, I would like to acknowledge God and thank Him for all He has done in my life and all He has brought me through. With God, I have come to an unshakable faith and hope for the future. The gift of faith in Jesus Christ is life changing. It brings hope.

I am indebted to the women who have so generously shared their own struggles and triumphs in the pages of this book, bravely sharing their stories to inspire and encourage others.

Thank you, Ann-Marie McCann, Jenni Sedon, Jill Sutcliffe Everett, Julie Mengel, Karene Gravener, Dr Rhonda Emonson, Ruth, Samantha Leonoski, Sharon Henderson, Soleil Nyirabyiza and Uma Rani Turimelli. Thank you for the trust you have placed in me as we have worked together to craft the chapters that represent each of your journeys. Thank you from the bottom of my heart for being a part of this process and this book.

I especially want to acknowledge the love and support of my family who have encouraged me in this journey as an author, again! To my husband, Daryl, and my children, Jessica, Danielle and Timothy – thank you!

For my friends who have been interested in and supportive of my book-writing venture – your words of encouragement have been timely. I would particularly like to acknowledge and thank those men and women of faith who have so generously given of their time to write a testimonial for this book: Emeritus Rev Emmanuel Fave, Senior Pastor Jo Geerling, Kara Martin, Kelly Markey, and Pastor Ulemu Nyasulu. I have been truly humbled and encouraged by what you have said.

To the excellent photography by Megan Marano of *Insight Creative Photography*, who captured some wonderful photos of me for my chapter and the back cover of this book – thank you.

To Natasa Denman and the publishing and mentoring team at *Ultimate 48 Hour Author*, thank you so much for your support, wisdom and guidance in the writing and publishing of this book. Your influence has made what seemed out of reach – writing this book – not only possible, but also enjoyable along the way. Thank you for investing your time and expertise in me.

I would also like to acknowledge the traditional custodians of the land on which I live and call home, the Wulgurukaba and Bindal people and pay my respects to their elders, past, present and emerging.

Speaker Bio

Dr Amanda Nickson is the author of *Hope for the Future, Inspiring Women's Stories Showing the Way*. A highly regarded speaker and teacher in her professional life as a social worker and pastor, Amanda has a PhD in Social Work and is recognised in her field as an expert in social work supervision.

An accomplished professional and engaging public speaker, Amanda focuses her passion to encourage and inspire others to live life to the full and not to be limited because of past or current circumstances or the limiting expectations of others.

Amanda shares a well-grounded perspective on the way forward for empowering women to step into their purpose and live with hope. She easily connects with her audiences leaving them motivated and inspired.

Amanda's keynotes, which can be customised to suit any audience, include:

1. **How to have hope despite difficult circumstances:**
    - Ways forward when life seems hopeless or impossible
    - Inspiration for going forward
    - Eternal perspectives on challenges and eternal hope

2. **Finding your purpose and creating your vision for the future:**
    - Finding your strengths and passions
    - Overcoming limiting beliefs
    - Creating goals for the future

3. **Being a partner in hope for others:**
    - Supporting and encouraging others needing hope
    - Motivation and inspiration
    - Opportunities to help others

To enquire about booking Amanda to speak at your conference, women's group, church or next event, email: *amanda@amandanickson.com.au*

More details at: *https://www.amandanickson.com.au/*

Offers

Offer 1

A free copy of Chapter 1 – available as a sampler as a PDF, which is great to share with others who may be interested. Available at *http://www.amandanickson.com.au/*

Offer 2

Finding Hope – a six-week online course. See Amanda's website at *http://www.amandanickson.com.au/* for details and mention this offer for a 20% discount.

Offer 3

Engage Dr Amanda Nickson as a speaker for you next Women's Conference, event, retreat or meeting. To enquire about booking Amanda to speak at your next event or for availabilities, email: *amanda@amandanickson.com.au*

www.ingramcontent.com/pod-product-compliance
Lightning Source LLC
Chambersburg PA
CBHW041141110526
44590CB00027B/4090